Lesson 1: **Numbers to 100**

- Count, read and write numbers to 100

M000168222

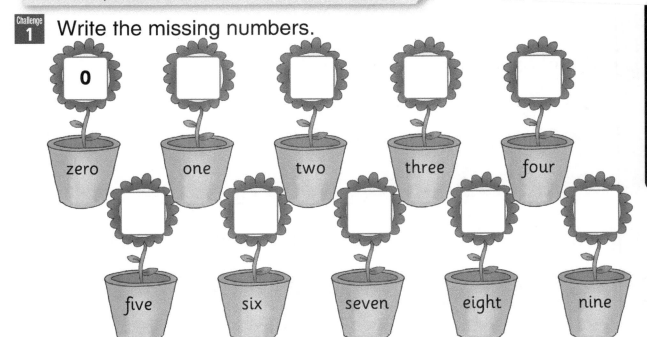

Challenge 1 Write the missing numbers.

0				
zero	one	two	three	four

five	six	seven	eight	nine

Challenge 2 Write the missing numbers.

10				
ten	twenty	thirty	forty	fifty

sixty	seventy	eighty	ninety	one hundred

Challenge 3 Draw lines to join each child to the right number.

14   65

fourteen

thirty-two

sixty-five

ninety-six

96   32

Number

1

Lesson 2: **Counting on and back in steps**

Number

• Count in 2s, 5s and 10s

Challenge 1 Count on in 2s to fill in the numbers.

2   4   ⬜   8   ⬜   12   ⬜

6   ⬜   10   12   ⬜   16   ⬜

Challenge 2 Count on in 5s or 10s and write the numbers in the boxes.

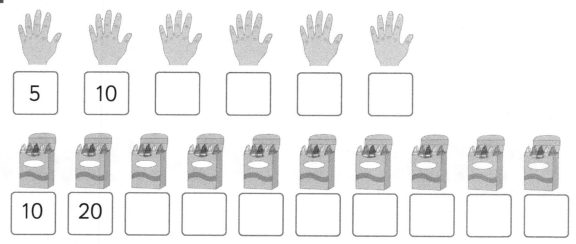

| 5 | 10 | | | | |

| 10 | 20 | | | | | | | | |

Challenge 3 Count back in 5s.

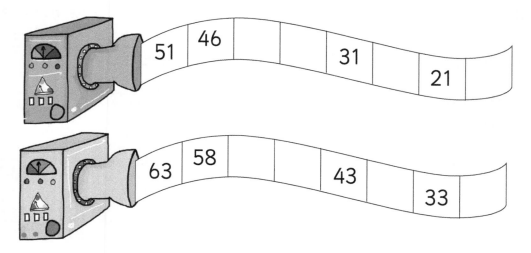

| 51 | 46 | | | 31 | | 21 | |

| 63 | 58 | | | 43 | | 33 | |

2

Collins

INTERNATIONAL PRIMARY MATHS

Workbook 2

William Collins' dream of knowledge for all began with the publication of his first book in 1819. A self-educated mill worker, he not only enriched millions of lives, but also founded a flourishing publishing house. Today, staying true to this spirit, Collins books are packed with inspiration, innovation and practical expertise. They place you at the centre of a world of possibility and give you exactly what you need to explore it.

Collins. Freedom to teach.

An imprint of HarperCollins*Publishers*
The News Building
1 London Bridge Street
London
SE1 9GF

HarperCollins *Publishers*
1st Floor
Watermarque Building
Ringsend Road
Dublin 4
Ireland

Browse the complete Collins catalogue at
www.collins.co.uk

12

ISBN 978-0-00-815985-6

British Library Cataloguing in Publication Data
A catalogue record for this publication is available from the British Library.

Commissioned by Fiona McGlade
Series editor Peter Clarke
Project editor Kate Ellis
Project managed by Emily Hooton
Developed by Joan Miller, Tracy Thomas and Karen Williams
Edited by Tanya Solomons
Proofread by Catherine Dakin
Cover design by Ink Tank
Cover artwork by Aflo Co. Ltd./Alamy Stock Photo
Internal design by Ken Vail Graphic Design
Typesetting by Ken Vail Graphic Design
Illustrations by Ken Vail Graphic Design, Advocate Art and Beehive Illustrations
Production by Lauren Crisp
Printed and Bound in the UK using 100% Renewable Electricity at CPI Group (UK) Ltd

MIX
Paper from
responsible sources
FSC
www.fsc.org   FSC™ C007454

Contents

Measure

Handling data

Lesson 3: **Counting many objects (1)**

- Count up to 100 objects
- Count objects in groups of 2, 5 or 10

Challenge 1

1 Count in 2s. Circle each set.

There are ☐ fish.

2 Count in 5s. Circle each set.

There are ☐ cakes.

Challenge 2

1 Count in 5s. Circle each set.   **2** Count in 10s. Circle each set.

There are ☐ sweets.   There are ☐ cars.

Challenge 3

Count in 10s. Circle each set.

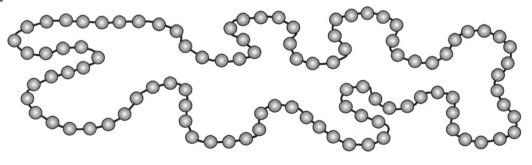

There are ☐ beads.

Lesson 4: **1 or 10 more or less**

- Find 1 or 10 more or less than a number

Challenge 1 Find 1 more than and 10 more than for each flower.

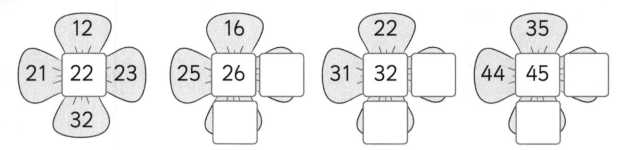

Challenge 2 **1** Find 1 less than and 10 less than for each flower.

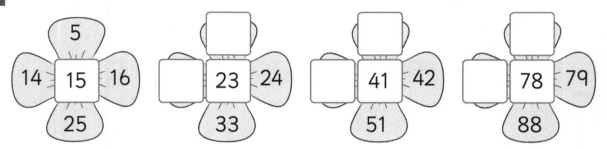

2 Fill in all the numbers on the petals.

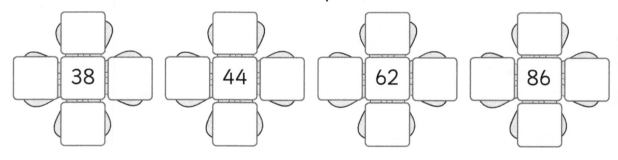

Challenge 3 Fill in the numbers on these flower number crosses.

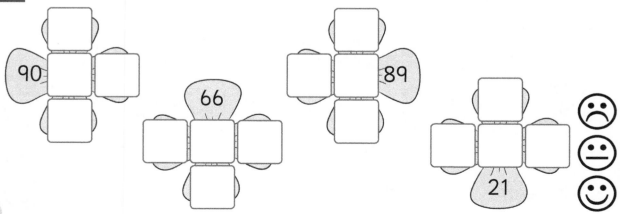

Lesson 5: **Finding numbers**

- Say a number that falls between 2 other numbers
- Place a 2-digit number on a number line

 Challenge 1 Write the numbers on the number line.

32, 36, 37

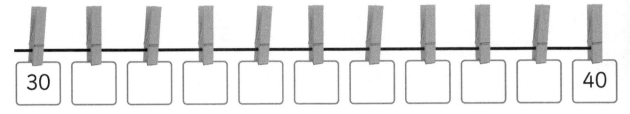

30 ☐ ☐ ☐ ☐ ☐ ☐ ☐ ☐ ☐ 40

Challenge 2 **1** Complete the number line.

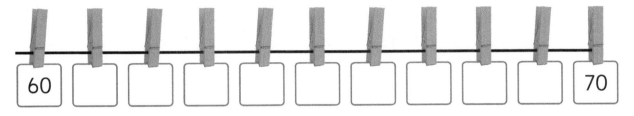

60 ☐ ☐ ☐ ☐ ☐ ☐ ☐ ☐ ☐ 70

2 Write each number on the number line.

a 44

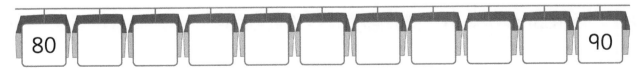

40 ☐ ☐ ☐ ☐ ☐ ☐ ☐ ☐ ☐ 50

b 81

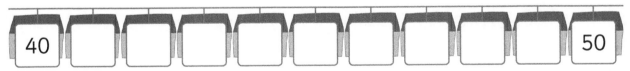

80 ☐ ☐ ☐ ☐ ☐ ☐ ☐ ☐ ☐ 90

Challenge 3 Write each number on the number line.

45, 32, 27

0   50

5

Lesson 6: **Rounding numbers (1)**

• Round 2-digit numbers to the nearest 10

Number

Challenge 1

Circle the 10 that each number rounds to.

a

30   **31**   40

b

50   **57**   60

Challenge 2

Write the number on the number line and circle the 10 that it rounds to.

a 69

60   70

b 43

40   50

c 72

70   80

Challenge 3

Do these numbers round up or down? Write the nearest 10.

16 rounds [up] to [30]   35 rounds [   ] to [   ]

14 rounds [   ] to [   ]   32 rounds [   ] to [   ]

95 rounds [   ] to [   ]   26 rounds [   ] to [   ]

Lesson 7: **Ordinal numbers**

• Use ordinal numbers

You will need
• coloured pencils

 Fill in the missing ordinal numbers to show the positions.

1st 2nd ☐ 4th ☐ ☐ 7th 8th ☐ 10th

1st ☐ ☐ ☐ ☐ ☐ ☐ ☐ ☐ ☐

a Colour the 7th flower blue.

b Colour the 10th flower red.

c Colour the 3rd flower yellow.

 1 Fill in the missing dates.

						1st	
3rd	4th		6th				9th
10th	11th	12th	13th	14th	15th	16th	
17th	18th	19th	20th	21st	22nd	23rd	
24th	25th	26th	27th	28th	29th	30th	

2 The day after the 11th is party day. Colour it red.

7

Lesson 8: **Odd and even numbers**

- Recognise odd and even numbers to 20

You will need
- coloured pencils

Number

Challenge 1 Colour the even numbers.

| 1 | 2 | 3 | 4 | 5 | 6 | 7 | 8 | 9 | 10 | 11 | 12 | 13 | 14 | 15 | 16 | 17 | 18 | 19 | 20 |

Challenge 2

1 Draw lines to join the boats to the odd or even bank.

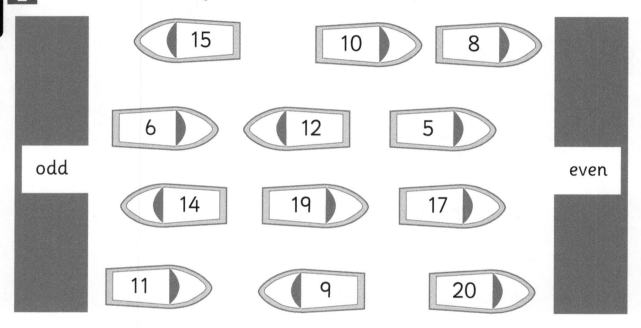

2 Circle the number that should not be in this group.

17, 13, 19, 14, 11

Challenge 3 Colour the odd numbers red and the even numbers blue.

27   29   18   15   26

30   22   13   24   21

Lesson 1: **Counting many objects (2)** Unit

- Count on and back in ones and tens
- Make groups of objects and count them in 2s, 5s and 10s

Challenge 1

1 Count the snails in groups of 2. ☐

2 Count the ladybirds in groups of 10. ☐

Challenge 2 Count the groups first and then count on in 1s to find the total.

a ● ● ● ● ● ●   ● ● ● ● ●   ● ● ● ● ●   ● ●   ☐

b ● ● ●   ● ●   ● ●   ● ●   ●   ☐

c ●●●●●● / ●●●●● / ●●●●●● / ●●   ☐

Challenge 3 Count out 27 counters in 1s.

Try grouping them in 2s, then 5s, then 10s.

Which was the best way of grouping them? Why?

• Know how many tens and ones are in a 2-digit number

Challenge 1

How many tens? How many ones?

a

tens: ☐   ones: ☐

b

tens: ☐   ones: ☐

Challenge 2

How many tens? How many ones?

a 57

tens: ones:

☐ ☐

b 19

tens: ones:

☐ ☐

c 61

tens: ones:

☐ ☐

d 95

tens: ones:

☐ ☐

e 44

tens: ones:

☐ ☐

f 28

tens: ones:

☐ ☐

Challenge 3

Write a 2-digit number. ☐

How many tens? ☐

How many ones? ☐

Draw cubes for your number.

Lesson 3: **Place value (2)**

• Partition 2-digit numbers into tens and ones

Challenge 1 Complete the partitioning.

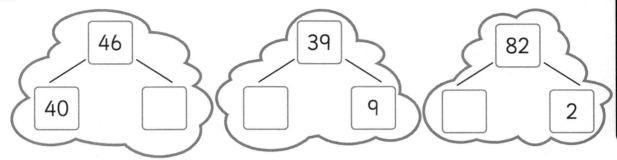

Challenge 2 Partition these numbers.

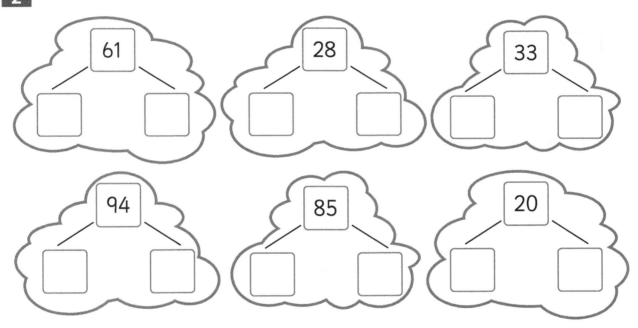

Challenge 3 Fill in the missing numbers.

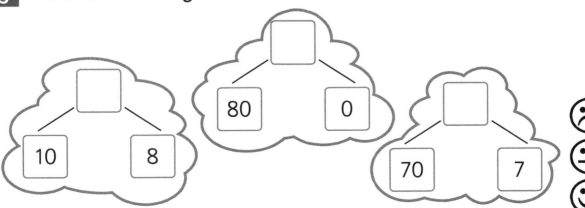

Lesson 4: **Comparing numbers**

Number

• Use the < and > signs to compare two numbers

Challenge 1 Write a number in the box to make each statement true.

a  20 < ☐

b  16 > ☐

c  27 > ☐

d 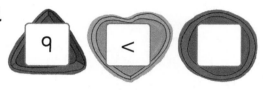 9 < ☐

Challenge 2 Compare the numbers and use < or >.

a  9 ☐ 10

b  22 ☐ 33

c  80 ☐ 50

d  84 ☐ 48

Challenge 3 Circle true or false.

a 10 + 5 < 18 True / False

b 35 < 12 + 7 True / False

c 17 + 3 > 50 True / False

12

Lesson 5: **Ordering numbers**

• Order numbers to 100

Challenge 1 Write the numbers in each set in order, smallest to largest.

a 18, 5, 12, 20

b 6, 10, 15, 17

Challenge 2 Write the numbers in each set in order, smallest to largest.

a 72, 24, 93, 16, 40

b 30, 81, 55, 69, 76

c 13, 99, 65, 22, 36

Challenge 3 Write the numbers in each set in order, largest to smallest.

a 56, 82, 38, 52, 90, 79, 71

b 29, 25, 60, 78, 20, 99, 92

Number

13

Lesson 6: **Rounding numbers (2)**

• Round 2-digit numbers to the nearest 10

Number

Challenge 1 Draw lines to show which 10 each number rounds to.

24   29
                        25
20   28
              23   27
                                        30

    22   21   26

Challenge 2 Round these numbers to the nearest 10.

41   77   62

98   85   38

1   56   83

Challenge 3 **1** Write six numbers that round to 70.

| | | | 70 | | | |

2 Write eight numbers that round to 50.

| | | | | 50 | | | | |

14

Lesson 7: **Estimating**

- Estimate 'how many' for up to 100 objects

Challenge 1 Circle how many you think there are.

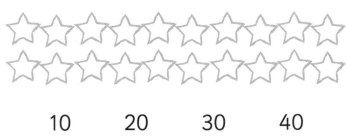

10   20   30   40

Challenge 2

1 Circle how many you think there are.

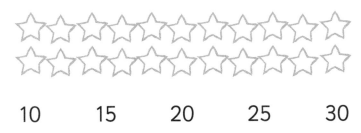

10   15   20   25   30

2 Circle how many you think there are.

35   40   45   50   55

Challenge 3 Circle how many you think there are.

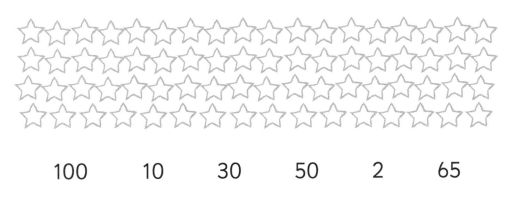

100   10   30   50   2   65

15

Number

• Sort numbers into groups

Challenge 1

Colour the multiples of 5.

1	2	3	4	5	6	7	8	9	10	11	12	13	14	15
16	17	18	19	20	21	22	23	24	25	26	27	28	29	30
31	32	33	34	35	36	37	38	39	40	41	42	43	44	45
46	47	48	49	50	51	52	53	54	55	56	57	58	59	60

Challenge 2

Join the numbers to greater than >20 or less than <20.

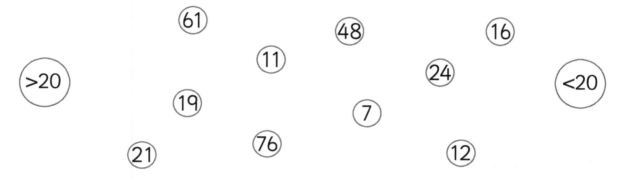

61   48   16

11   24

>20   19   24   <20

7

76   12

21   12

Challenge 3

1 Circle the two numbers that have been sorted incorrectly.

odd
13   92   61
53   7

even
2   83   58
70   16

2 Circle the two numbers that have been sorted incorrectly.

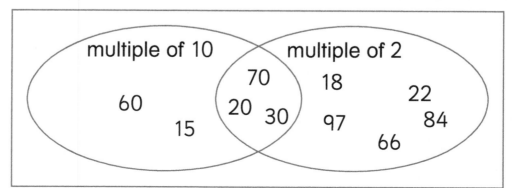

multiple of 10   multiple of 2
70   18
60   20   30   22
15   97   84
66

Lesson 1: **Counting in 2s, 5s and 10s**

- Make and continue number patterns by counting in 2s, 5s and 10s

Challenge 1 Continue the number patterns.

a 2 4 6 8 10 ☆ ☆ ☆

b 10 20 30 40 50 ☆ ☆ ☆

Challenge 2

1 Continue the number patterns.

a 10 15 20 25 ◻ ◻ ◻

b 16 14 12 10 8 ◻ ◻ ◻

2 Circle the answers in this sentence.

The pattern on the trees is counting **on / back** in: **2s / 5s / 10s**.

30   25   20   15   10

Challenge 3 Continue the number patterns.

a 34 44 54 64 ◻ ◻ ◻ ◻

The pattern is counting on in: ◻

b 12 17 22 27 32 ◻ ◻ ◻

The pattern is counting on in: ◻

17

• Count on in small constant steps

Challenge 1

1 Colour the numbers you say when you count in 3s.

| 1 | 2 | 3 | 4 | 5 | 6 | 7 | 8 | 9 | 10 | 11 | 12 | 13 | 14 | 15 | 16 | 17 | 18 | 19 | 20 |

2 Colour the numbers you say when you count in 4s.

| 1 | 2 | 3 | 4 | 5 | 6 | 7 | 8 | 9 | 10 | 11 | 12 | 13 | 14 | 15 | 16 | 17 | 18 | 19 | 20 |

Challenge 2

1 Skip-count the cherries in 3s.

a  ☐

b  ☐

2 Skip-count the orange segments in 6s.

a  ☐

b  ☐

Challenge 3

1 Count in 3s. What numbers come next?

9   12   15   18   ☐   ☐   ☐   ☐

2 Count in 7s. What numbers come next?

14   21   28   35   ☐   ☐   ☐

Lesson 3: **Place value (3)**

- Write a number sentence to partition a 2-digit number

Challenge 1 Write the missing numbers.

a 12 + | 10 | = 22

b [ ] + 15 = 16

c 25 + [ ] = 28

Challenge 2 Write the missing numbers.

a 29 = 20 + [ ]

b 71 = 70 + [ ]

c 68 = [ ] + 8

d 15 = [ ] + 5

e [ ] = 30 + 2

f [ ] = 40 + 0

g 43 = 40 + [ ]

h 79 = [ ] + 7

Challenge 3 Write partitioning number sentences for these numbers.

a 47 = [ ] + [ ]

b 25 = [ ] + [ ]

c 92 = [ ] + [ ]

d 75 = [ ] + [ ]

e 84 = [ ] + [ ]

f 69 = [ ] + [ ]

Lesson 4: **Comparing and ordering numbers (2)**

Unit **3**

Number

- Use the $<$ and $>$ signs to compare two numbers
- Put numbers to 100 in order

Challenge 1

Which of the numbers belong in the empty box?

a 10   8   28

$18 < \boxed{}$

b 60   93   90

$83 > \boxed{}$

c 21   32   19

$23 < \boxed{}$

d 36   32   17

$\boxed{} > 33$

Challenge 2

1 Write these numbers in order, from smallest to largest.

52, 20, 81, 83, 12, 38

$\boxed{}\ \boxed{}\ \boxed{}\ \boxed{}\ \boxed{}\ \boxed{}$

2 Write these numbers in order, from largest to smallest.

52, 20, 81, 83, 12, 38

$\boxed{}\ \boxed{}\ \boxed{}\ \boxed{}\ \boxed{}\ \boxed{}$

Challenge 3

Tick the box if the sign is correct.

a $67 < 97$ $\boxed{}$

b $4 > 44$ $\boxed{}$

c $95 > 99$ $\boxed{}$

d $25 < 43$ $\boxed{}$

Lesson 1: **Halves**

- Write one half as $\frac{1}{2}$
- Recognise shapes that are divided into halves and shapes that are not

Challenge 1 Colour the shapes that are in halves.

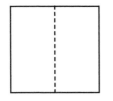 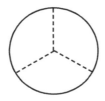  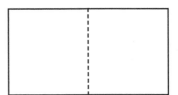

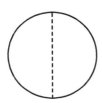 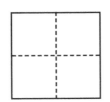  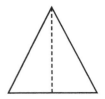

Challenge 2 Colour the shapes that are divided into halves, then label each half $\frac{1}{2}$.

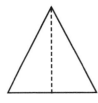 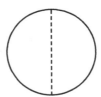 

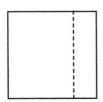  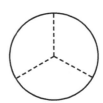

Challenge 3 Colour the shapes that have been labelled correctly.

 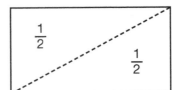

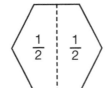 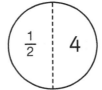

Lesson 2: **Quarters**

- Write one quarter as $\frac{1}{4}$
- Recognise which shapes are divided into quarters and which are not

Number

Challenge 1 Colour the shapes that are divided into quarters.

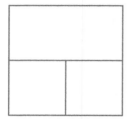

Challenge 2 Colour the shapes that are divided into quarters, then label each quarter $\frac{1}{4}$.

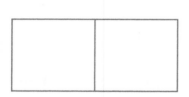

Challenge 3 Colour the shapes that have been labelled correctly.

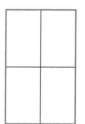 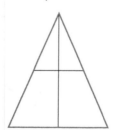 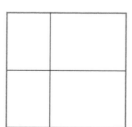 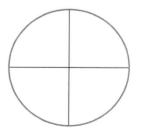 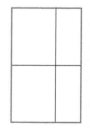

Lesson 3: **Three quarters**

- Recognise and write $\frac{3}{4}$

Challenge 1 Tick the shapes that show three quarters shaded.

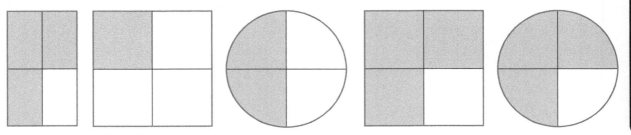

Challenge 2 Tick the shapes that show three quarters shaded.
Write $\frac{3}{4}$ next to the shapes that are correctly shaded.

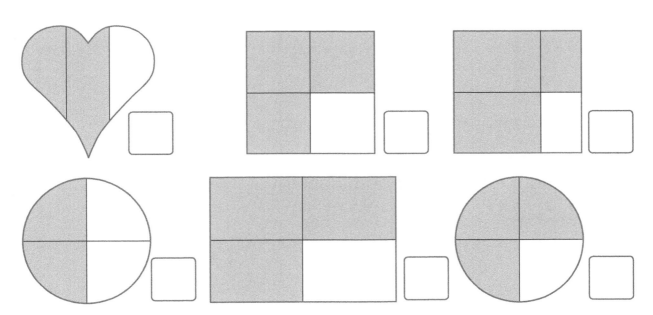

Challenge 3 Divide these shapes into quarters. Colour $\frac{3}{4}$ of the shape.

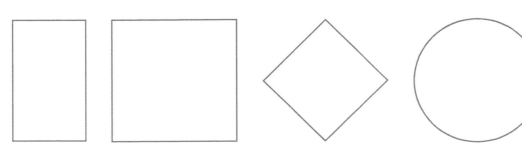

Lesson 4: **Halves and quarters of shapes**

• Find halves and quarters of shapes

Challenge 1

1 Colour one half.

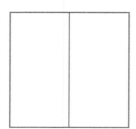

2 Colour one quarter.

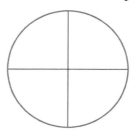

Challenge 2

1 Use a pencil and ruler to divide each shape into halves. Colour one half and label it $\frac{1}{2}$.

  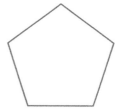

2 Use a pencil and ruler to find one quarter of each shape. Colour one quarter and label it $\frac{1}{4}$.

 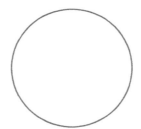 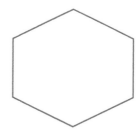

Challenge 3

Find two different ways of dividing a square into quarters. Then colour one quarter of each square and label it $\frac{1}{4}$.

Lesson 5: **Making a whole**

- Recognise that $\frac{2}{2}$ and $\frac{4}{4}$ both make a whole

Challenge 1 Colour the circles that are equal to one whole.

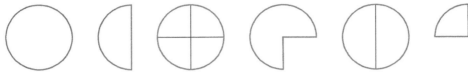

Challenge 2 **1** How many halves must be shaded to make one whole?

a 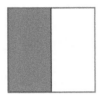 □

b □

2 How many quarters must be shaded to make one whole?

a 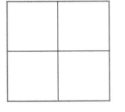 □

b  □

c 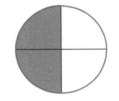 □

d 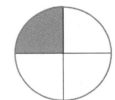 □

Challenge 3 **1** How many whole ovals can you make from these halves?

□

2 How many whole squares can you make from these quarters?

□

25

Lesson 6: **Equal fractions**

- Recognise that $\frac{1}{2}$ and $\frac{2}{4}$ are the same

Challenge 1 Colour one half of each shape.

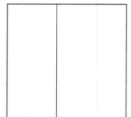
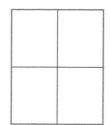
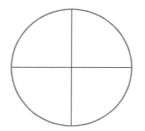
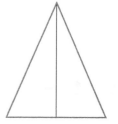

Challenge 2 Tick the shapes that have an equal fraction shaded.

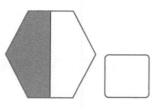
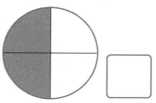
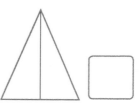

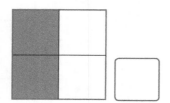
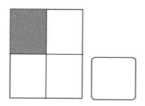
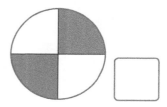

Challenge 3 Circle the shapes which have an equal fraction shaded.

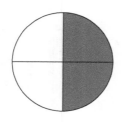
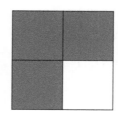
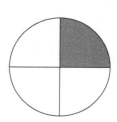

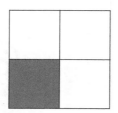

Lesson 7: **Halves of numbers of objects**

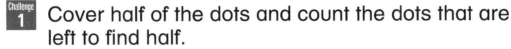

• Find halves of small numbers of objects

Challenge 1 Cover half of the dots and count the dots that are left to find half.

a

b

c

Challenge 2 Cross out half of the pictures to solve these problems.

a

James has 6 stars. He gives half to his brother. How many does he have left?

b

There are 14 grapes. Anna eats half of them. How many are left?

Challenge 3 Draw a picture to help you to solve this problem.

There are 16 butterflies in a tree.
Half fly to a bush. How many are left?

Number

27

Lesson 8: **Quarters of numbers of objects**

• Find one quarter of small numbers of objects

Challenge 1 How many stars are in each quarter?

a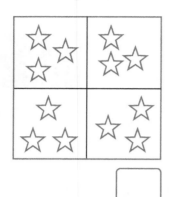

b

c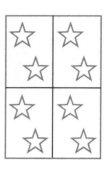

Challenge 2 Draw dots in each quarter to find one quarter.

a 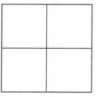 There are 12 children. A quarter of them go to the cinema. How many children is that?

b 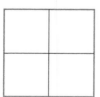 Asim has 8 pets. One quarter of his pets are rabbits. How many rabbits does Asim have?

c Priya has 20 strawberries. Her mum says she may eat a quarter of them. How many strawberries is Priya allowed to eat?

Challenge 3 Write a number story to match this number sentence, then work out the answer.

$\frac{1}{4}$ of 16 = ☐ _____

_____

_____

• Know all the number pairs for 10 and 20

 1 Draw extra dots to make 20 and complete the number bonds.

a

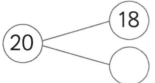

b

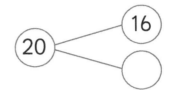

 2 Complete the number bonds for 20.

a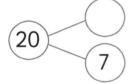

b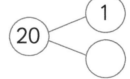

c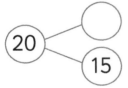

d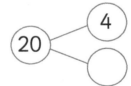

 **3** Write five different number bonds for 20.

Number

- Find number bonds for a number from 10 to 20
- Write number sentences to match these number bonds

Challenge 1

Find ways of making 15. Then write number sentences.

a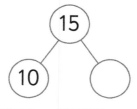

b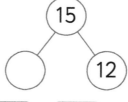

c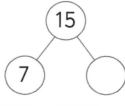

10 + ☐ = 15   ☐ + ☐ = 15   ☐ + ☐ = 15

Challenge 2

1 Draw lines to match the pairs of numbers that make 16.

| 9 | 3 | 15 | 5 | 8 | 12 |

| 11 | 7 | 4 | 13 | 1 | 8 |

2 Finish the number sentences for this bond.

$11 +$ ☐ $= 15$ ☐ $+$ ☐ $= 15$

$15 -$ ☐ $= 11$ ☐ $- 11 = 4$

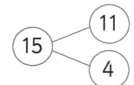

Challenge 3

1 Write as many pairs of numbers that make 17 as you can.

17 ☐

2 Choose one of the number pairs and write four facts to match it.

☐ ☐ ☐ ☐

Number

• Find pairs of multiples of 10 that make 100

Challenge 1 Complete the number bonds for 100.

a
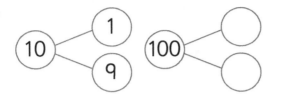

b
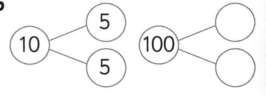

c
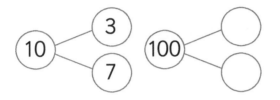

d
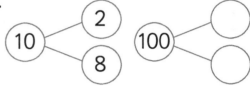

Challenge 2

1 Write the multiple of 10 to make 100.

40 + ☐   30 + ☐   10 + ☐   0 + ☐

2 Write an addition and a subtraction fact for each number bond.

a

b

Challenge 3

1 Write four pairs of multiples of 10 that total 100.

2 Choose one of your pairs and write four facts to match it.

Lesson 4: **The equals sign (=)**

• Use the = sign to show that two number statements are equal

Challenge 1 Finish the number statements to make the statement true.

a

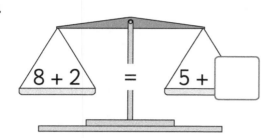

$8 + 2$ = $5 +$ ☐

b

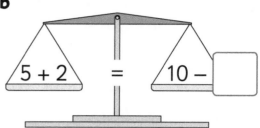

$5 + 2$ = $10 -$ ☐

Challenge 2 Write a number sentence to make each statement true.

a

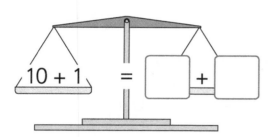

$10 + 1$ = ☐ + ☐

b

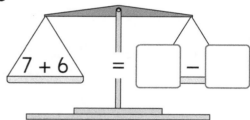

$7 + 6$ = ☐ − ☐

c d

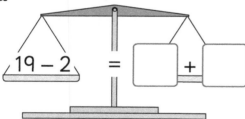

$19 - 2$ = ☐ + ☐

$8 + 7$ = ☐ − ☐

Challenge 3 Write two different number sentences for each number.

a 18   ☐ + ☐ = ☐ − ☐

b 20   ☐ − ☐ = ☐ + ☐

c 14   ☐ + ☐ = ☐ + ☐

d 16   ☐ − ☐ = ☐ + ☐

Lesson 5: **Adding more than two numbers**

• Add more than two small numbers together

 1 5 + 2 + 1 = ☐   **2** 4 + 3 + 2 = ☐   **3** 6 + 4 + 3 = ☐

 Order the numbers, then add them together.

a 3 + 4 + 1 + 2

☐ + ☐ + ☐ + ☐ = ☐

b 7 + 5 + 1 + 3

☐ + ☐ + ☐ + ☐ = ☐

c 1 + 2 + 3 + 4 + 5

☐ + ☐ + ☐ + ☐ + ☐ = ☐

Write the number sentence, then add the numbers together. Use a number line to help.

a I bought 2 teddies, 8 marbles, 3 cars, 10 stickers and 1 ball. How many things did I buy?

☐ + ☐ + ☐ + ☐ + ☐ = ☐

b I saw 5 spiders, 4 ladybirds, 11 ants, 1 beetle and 3 snails. How many minibeasts did I see?

☐ + ☐ + ☐ + ☐ + ☐ = ☐

Lesson 6: **Adding a single-digit number to a 2-digit number (1)**

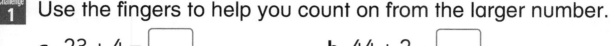

• Add a single digit to a 2-digit number by counting on

Challenge 1 Use the fingers to help you count on from the larger number.

a 23 + 4 = ☐

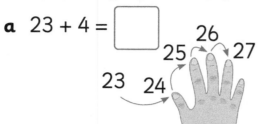

26
25   27
23   24

b 44 + 2 = ☐

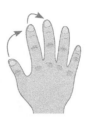

c 17 + 5 = ☐

d 35 + 8 = ☐

Challenge 2 Solve by counting on from the larger number.

a 62 + 7 = ☐   **b** 15 + 8 = ☐

c 5 + 38 = ☐   **d** 23 + 6 = ☐

e 71 + 7 = ☐   **f** 88 + 4 = ☐

Challenge 3 Solve by counting on from the larger number.

a There are 27 learners in a class. 6 new learners join.
How many learners are in the class now?

☐ + ☐ = ☐

b Dad bakes 36 cakes. He needs to bake 9 more.
How many cakes must he bake altogether?

☐ + ☐ = ☐

Lesson 7: **Subtracting a single-digit number from a 2-digit number (1)**

• Subtract a single digit from a 2-digit number by counting back

Challenge 1 Use the fingers to help you count back from the larger number.

a 29 – 5 = ☐

b 15 – 6 = ☐

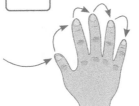
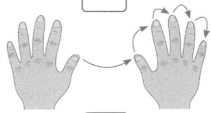

c 78 – 7 = ☐

d 56 – 9 = ☐

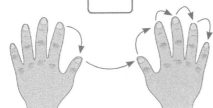
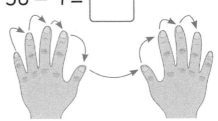

Challenge 2 Solve by counting back from the larger number.

a Adam has 50c. He buys a sticker for 8c. How much money does he have left?

☐ – ☐ = ☐

b Eve invited 19 children to a party, but 3 of them can't come. How many children can come to the party?

☐ – ☐ = ☐

Challenge 3 Write a number story to match this number sentence, then work out the answer: 64 – 8 = ☐

_____

_____

_____

_____

Lesson 8: **In any order?**

- Understand that addition can be done in any order but that subtraction cannot

Number

Challenge 1 Work out each answer, then add the numbers in a different order.

a

7 + 3 = ☐   ☐ + 7 = ☐

b

12 + 6 = ☐   ☐ + 12 = ☐

Challenge 2 Tick (✓) the calculations which are correct.

a 9 + 5 is the same as 5 + 9 ☐

b 9 – 5 is the same as 5 – 9 ☐

c 13 + 15 is the same as 15 + 13 ☐

d 7 – 6 is the same as 6 – 7 ☐

Challenge 3

1 Find as many different ways as you can to order the numbers in this addition.

13 + 7 + 5 = ☐   ☐

2 How many different ways can you order the numbers in this subtraction to get the same answer?

15 – 5 + 10   ☐

☹
😐
☺

Lesson 1: **Addition and subtraction bonds to 20 (2)**

- Find number bonds for numbers to 20 and write additions and subtractions to match

Challenge 1 Write two pairs of numbers that total 13.

 **a** 11 and ☐   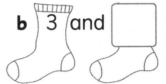 **b** 3 and ☐

Challenge 2 **1** Write three pairs of numbers that total 16.

☐ and ☐   ☐ and ☐   ☐ and ☐

2 Choose one of the pairs from Question 1 and write one addition and one subtraction to match it.

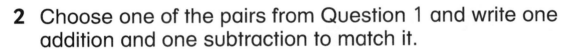
☐ + ☐ = 16   16 − ☐ = ☐

Challenge 3 **1** Write three pairs of numbers that total 19.

☐ and ☐   ☐ and ☐   ☐ and ☐

2 Choose one of the pairs from Question 1 and write two additions and two subtractions to match it.

☐ + ☐ = ☐   ☐ + ☐ = ☐

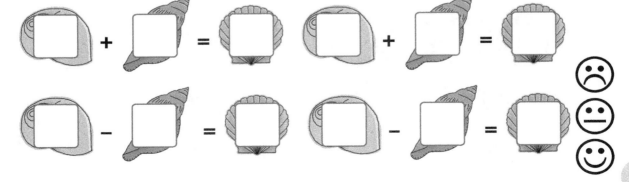
☐ − ☐ = ☐   ☐ − ☐ = ☐

Lesson 2: **Adding tens to a 2-digit number**

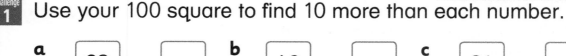

* Add multiples of 10 to a 2-digit number

You will need
* 100 square

Challenge 1

Use your 100 square to find 10 more than each number.

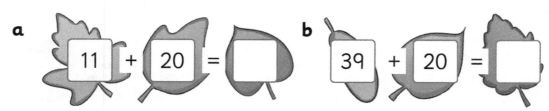

a 28   b 63   c 81

Challenge 2

Solve these additions by counting on in tens on your 100 square.

a 11 + 20 =   b 39 + 20 =

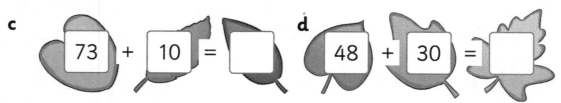

c 73 + 10 =   d 48 + 30 =

Challenge 3

Estimate the answer, then solve by counting on in tens.

a 25 + 70 =   b 42 + 50 =

Estimate: ☐   Estimate: ☐

Answer: ☐   Answer: ☐

c 11 + 80 =   d 36 + 40 =

Estimate: ☐   Estimate: ☐

Answer: ☐   Answer: ☐

Lesson 3: **Adding a single-digit number to a 2-digit number (2)**

- Add a single-digit number to a 2-digit number

You will need
- 100 square

 Challenge 1 Find the 2-digit number on your 100 square and count on.

a $44 + 7 = \boxed{}$ **b** $38 + 8 = \boxed{}$ **c** $86 + 9 = \boxed{}$

 Challenge 2 Write the number sentence and solve the problem.

a

34 books add 5 more equals how many?

_____

_____

b

67 coins plus 4 more makes how many?

_____

_____

c
18 sweets and 4 sweets makes how many altogether?

_____

_____

d
78 cars add 4 more cars equals how many?

_____

_____

 Challenge 3 Write the number sentence and solve the problem.

a There are 96 people on a train. Five more people got on. How many people are on the train now?

_____

b There are 94 flowers in the garden. Nadia planted 9 more. How many flowers are there now?

_____

Lesson 4: **Adding pairs of 2-digit numbers (2)**

• Use partitioning to add pairs of 2-digit numbers

Challenge 1

1

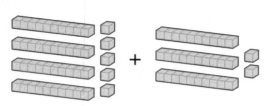

□ + □ = □

2

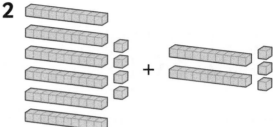

□ + □ = □

Challenge 2 Use Base 10 to solve these problems.

a 54 + 12 = □

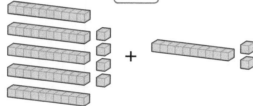

b 23 + 36 = □

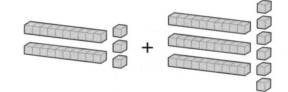

c 71 + 28 = □

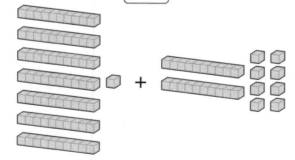

d 55 + 33 = □

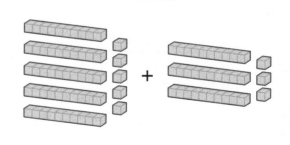

Challenge 3 Use Base 10 to solve these problems.

a 34 + 37 = □

b 28 + 36 = □

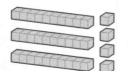 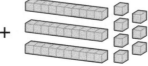 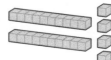 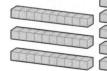

Lesson 5: 'Take away' and 'difference'

- Solve a subtraction by taking away or finding the difference

Challenge 1 Take away the smaller number from the larger number by counting back.

a $8 - 3 = \boxed{}$ **b** $10 - 6 = \boxed{}$ **c** $11 - 6 = \boxed{}$

Challenge 2 Find the difference between these numbers by counting on from the smaller number to the larger number.

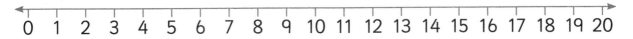

0 1 2 3 4 5 6 7 8 9 10 11 12 13 14 15 16 17 18 19 20

a $17 - 14 = \boxed{}$ **b** $14 - 9 = \boxed{}$

c $16 - 8 = \boxed{}$ **d** $15 - 10 = \boxed{}$

e $13 - 9 = \boxed{}$ **f** $20 - 3 = \boxed{}$

Challenge 3 Work out the answer to each subtraction. Then circle the method you used.

a $16 - 12 = \boxed{}$

take away

find the difference

b $20 - 17 = \boxed{}$

take away

find the difference

c $15 - 3 = \boxed{}$

take away

find the difference

d $16 - 5 = \boxed{}$

take away

find the difference

Lesson 6: **Subtracting tens from a 2-digit number**

Number

- Subtract multiples of 10 from a 2-digit number

You will need
- 100 square

Challenge 1

Use your 100 square to find 10 less than each number.

a 95 ☐

b 21 ☐

c 47 ☐

d 78 ☐

41	42	43	44	45	46	47	48	49	50
51	52	53	54	55	56	57	58	59	60
61	62	63	64	65	66	67	68	69	70
71	72	73	74	75	76	77	78	79	80
81	82	83	84	85	86	87	88	89	90
91	92	93	94	(95)	96	97	98	99	100

Challenge 2

Solve these subtractions by counting back in tens.

a $32 - 10 =$ ☐

b $72 - 20 =$ ☐

c $66 - 30 =$ ☐

d $58 - 30 =$ ☐

Challenge 3

Solve these subtractions by counting back in tens.

a $99 - 80 =$ ☐

b $93 - 90 =$ ☐

c $74 - 50 =$ ☐

d $86 - 50 =$ ☐

e $71 - 40 =$ ☐

f $82 - 70 =$ ☐

Lesson 7: **Subtracting a single-digit number from a 2-digit number (2)**

• Subtract a single-digit number from a 2-digit number

Challenge 1 Count back from the 2-digit number to solve the subtraction.

20 21 22 23 24 25 26 27 28 29 30 31 32 33 34 35 36 37 38 39 40

a 37 − 5 = ☐   **b** 33 − 6 = ☐   **c** 31 − 4 = ☐

Challenge 2 Find the 2-digit number on your 100 square and count back to solve the subtraction.

a 61 − 7 = ☐   **b** 14 − 6 = ☐

c 73 − 9 = ☐   **d** 99 − 9 = ☐

Challenge 3

1 Jules collected 32 shells. Ana collected 7 fewer shells. How many shells did Ana collect? ☐

2 Last year, there were 45 people at the party. This year there were 9 fewer. How many people were at the party this year? ☐

43

• Find the difference between two numbers

You will need
• 100 square

Challenge 1

Find the difference. Start on the smaller number and count on until you reach the larger number.

60	61	62	63	64	65	66	67	68	69	70

a 62 and 65 ☐   **b** 60 and 64 ☐   **c** 64 and 69 ☐

Challenge 2

Use your 100 square to find the difference. Decide whether you want to start on the smaller or the larger number.

a 26 and 29 ☐   **b** 15 and 10 ☐

25	26	27	28	29	30

10	11	12	13	14	15

c 97 and 95 ☐   **d** 39 and 33 ☐

94	95	96	97	98	99

33	34	35	36	37	38	39

Challenge 3

Find the difference between each pair of numbers. Use the 100 square if you need to.

a $72 - 65 =$ ☐   **b** $43 - 35 =$ ☐

c $83 - 74 =$ ☐   **d** $95 - 91 =$ ☐

e $37 - 33 =$ ☐   **f** $55 - 49 =$ ☐

Lesson 1: **Addition and subtraction**

- Find number bonds for numbers to 20 and write additions and subtractions to match

Challenge 1 Write two pairs of numbers that make 14.

Challenge 2 **1** Write two pairs of numbers that make 18.

2 Now use the same numbers in these subtractions.

Challenge 3 Choose any number from 10 to 20.

Write additions facts for your number here.	Write related subtraction facts for your number here.

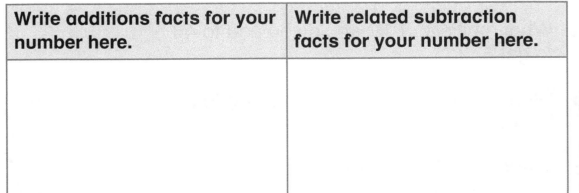

45

Lesson 2: **Adding and subtracting tens to and from a 2-digit number**

- Add and subtract multiples of 10 to and from a 2-digit number

Number (sidebar)

 Challenge 1

1 20 more than 72. ☐   **2** 30 more than 25.

3 20 less than 49. ☐   **4** 20 less than 58.

71	(72)	73	74	75	76	77	78	79	80
81	82	83	84	85	86	87	88	89	90
91	(92)	93	94	95	96	97	98	99	100

Challenge 2 Use your 100 square to solve these problems.

a $23 + 40 =$ ☐   **b** $44 - 40 =$ ☐

c $81 - 30 =$ ☐   **d** $19 + 20 =$ ☐

e $63 + 10 =$ ☐   **f** $74 - 50 =$ ☐

Challenge 3 Use your 100 square to solve these problems.

a What multiple of 10 would you add to 43 to get 63?

b What multiple of 10 would you add to 37 to get 77? ☐

c What multiple of 10 would you subtract from 76 to get 46? ☐

46

Lesson 3: **Adding and subtracting single-digit numbers**

• Add and subtract a single-digit number to and from a 2-digit number

Challenge 1 Answer these. Use counters to help you.

   a $14 + 4 = \boxed{}$ **b** $12 - 5 = \boxed{}$ **c** $28 - 4 = \boxed{}$

Challenge 2 Which strategy would you use to answer these? Join each calculation to the right strategy.

   a $32 + 3 = \boxed{}$

   b $26 - 7 = \boxed{}$

   c $64 + 5 = \boxed{}$

   d $98 - 6 = \boxed{}$

> $6 - 6$ and one more.

> $8 - 6$ is 2.

> $4 + 5$ is 9.

> $2 + 3$ is 5.

Challenge 3 Answer these. Show how you worked out the answer.

   a $29 + 6 = \boxed{}$

> 30 add 6 makes 36. Then take away 1 equals 35.

   b $48 - 9 = \boxed{}$

   c $34 + 6 = \boxed{}$

   d $17 - 12 = \boxed{}$

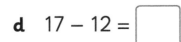

Lesson 4: **Adding pairs of 2-digit numbers (1)**

- Use partitioning to add pairs of 2-digit numbers

You will need
- 100 square

Challenge 1

Work out the answer by partitioning.

$37 + 22 = ?$

Add the tens:

$30 + 20 =$ ☐

Add the ones:

$7 + 2 =$ △

Add together

$50 + 9 =$ ◯

Challenge 2

Add these pairs of partitioned numbers together.
Use your 100 square.

a $35 + 23 =$ 35 + 23 = ☐

30 + 5 + 20 + 3 = ☐

b $41 + 57 =$ 41 + 57 = ☐

40 + 1 + 50 + 7 = ☐

c $72 + 14 =$ 72 + 14 = ☐

70 + 2 + 10 + 4 = ☐

Challenge 3

Use partitioning to add these pairs of numbers. Use your 100 square.

a $46 + 33 =$ ☐

b $65 + 24 =$ ☐

48

Lesson 5: **Adding pairs of 2-digit numbers (3)**

- Use partitioning to add pairs of 2-digit numbers

Challenge 1 Partition the numbers into tens and ones to add them together.

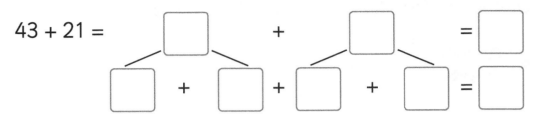

$$43 + 21 = \boxed{} + \boxed{} = \boxed{}$$

$$\boxed{} + \boxed{} + \boxed{} + \boxed{} = \boxed{}$$

Challenge 2 Write the number sentence and solve the problem.

a There were 24 birds in a tree. Twelve more joined them. How many birds are there now?

b Sumi picked 51 raspberries. Her brother picked 36. How many did they pick altogether?

Challenge 3 Write the number sentence and solve the problem.

a Irene's mum bought 23 carrots and 18 potatoes. How many vegetables did she buy?

b Roaul has 55c in his money box and 37c in his wallet. How much money does Roaul have?

Lesson 6: **Missing number problems (addition)**

- Find the missing number in an addition number sentence

You will need
- 100 square

Challenge 1

Use your 100 square to find the missing number of dots.

a ⚫⚫⚫ + ▢ = ⚪⚪⚪
⚫⚫⚫   ⚪⚪⚪
              ⚪⚪⚪

b ⚫ + ▢ = ⚪⚪⚪
⚫   ⚪⚪⚪⚪ ⚪

c ▢ + ⚫⚫ = ⚪⚪⚪⚪
      ⚫⚫   ⚪⚪⚪⚪

Challenge 2

Find the missing numbers.

a 14 + ▢ = 22   b 8 + ▢ = 16

c ▢ + 19 = 24   d ▢ + 7 = 13

Challenge 3

Find the missing numbers.

a 65 + ▢ = 74   b ▢ + 44 = 52

c ▢ + 21 = 26   d 36 + ▢ = 76

50

Lesson 7: **Missing number problems (subtraction)**

- Find the missing number in a subtraction number sentence

Challenge 1 Use your fingers or a 100 square to find the missing number.

a $\boxed{10} - \boxed{} = \boxed{3}$ **b** $\boxed{7} - \boxed{} = \boxed{2}$

c $\boxed{} - \boxed{5} = \boxed{7}$ **d** $\boxed{20} - \boxed{} = \boxed{9}$

Challenge 2 Find the missing number.

a $\boxed{19} - \boxed{} = \boxed{14}$ **b** $\boxed{13} - \boxed{} = \boxed{10}$

c $\boxed{} - \boxed{4} = \boxed{11}$ **d** $\boxed{} - \boxed{6} = \boxed{25}$

Challenge 3 Find the missing number.

a $\boxed{92} - \boxed{} = \boxed{84}$ **b** $\boxed{} - \boxed{6} = \boxed{73}$

c $\boxed{71} - \boxed{} = \boxed{62}$ **d** $\boxed{} - \boxed{40} = \boxed{36}$

e $\boxed{88} - \boxed{} = \boxed{18}$ **f** $\boxed{67} - \boxed{} = \boxed{59}$

Lesson 8: **Finding the difference (2)**

- Find the difference between two numbers

Challenge 1

Count on or back on the number line to find the difference.

a 42 and 47 ☐   **b** 58 and 55 ☐

40 41 42 43 44 45 46 47 48 49 50 51 52 53 54 55 56 57 58 59 60

Challenge 2

Count on or back on the number line to find the difference.
Draw a jump for each number.

a 33 and 37 ☐   **b** 48 and 43 ☐

30 31 32 33 34 35 36 37 38 39 40 41 42 43 44 45 46 47 48 49 50

Challenge 3

Count on or back on the number line to find the difference.
Draw a jump for each number.

a 68 and 73 ☐

b 21 and 17 ☐

52

Lesson 1: **Multiplying numbers**

- Use the × sign
- Understand multiplication as an array

Challenge 1 Complete the array to match the number sentence.

a 2 × 5

b 3 × 4

Challenge 2 Write two number facts for each array.

Challenge 3 Join each array to the matching calculation and find the answer.

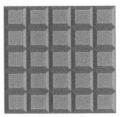

5 × 5 = ☐

3 × 6 = ☐

3 × 4 = ☐

2 × 10 = ☐

53

Lesson 2: **The 2 times table**

Number

- Recognise multiples of 2
- Use an array to recall 2 times table facts

Challenge 1 Colour the multiples of 2.

| 1 | 2 | 3 | 4 | 5 | 6 | 7 | 8 | 9 | 10 | 11 | 12 | 13 | 14 | 15 | 16 | 17 | 18 | 19 | 20 |

Challenge 2 Draw lines to match each 2 times table fact and answer.
Draw an array if you need to.

| 10 | 2 | 14 | 18 | 12 |

| 4 × 2 | 9 × 2 | 2 × 2 | 6 × 2 | 3 × 2 |

| 7 × 2 | 8 × 2 | 10 × 2 | 1 × 2 | 5 × 2 |

| 6 | 4 | 16 | 20 | 8 |

Challenge 3 Which 2 times table facts are these arrays showing?

a ☐ × 2 = ☐

b ☐ × 2 = ☐

c ☐ × 2 = ☐

d ☐ × 2 = ☐

Lesson 3: **The 5 times table**

- Recognise multiples of 5
- Use an array to recall 5 times table facts

Challenge 1 Continue counting in 5s to 50.

| 5 | 10 | | | | | | | | 50 |

Challenge 2 Draw a line to match each 5 times table fact and answer.
Draw an array if you need to.

| 10 | 25 | 30 | 35 | 50 |

| 4 × 5 | 9 × 5 | 2 × 5 | 6 × 5 | 3 × 5 |

| 7 × 5 | 8 × 5 | 10 × 5 | 1 × 5 | 5 × 5 |

| 15 | 5 | 45 | 20 | 40 |

Challenge 3 Which 5 times table facts are these arrays showing?

a  ☐ × 5 = ☐   b ☐ × 5 = ☐

55

Lesson 4: **The 10 times table**

- Recognise multiples of 10
- Use an array to recall 10 times table facts

Challenge 1 Continue counting in 10s to 100.

10 **20** ☐ ☐ ☐ ☐ ☐ ☐ ☐ ☐

Challenge 2 Draw lines to match each 10 times table fact and answer.
Draw an array if you need to.

| 10 | 80 | 100 | 50 | 30 |

| 4 × 10 | 9 × 10 | 2 × 10 | 6 × 10 | 3 × 10 |

| 7 × 10 | 8 × 10 | 10 × 10 | 1 × 10 | 5 × 10 |

| 60 | 20 | 70 | 90 | 40 |

Challenge 3 Which 10 times table facts are these arrays showing?

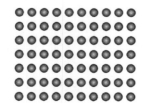

a ☐ × 10 = ☐   **b** ☐ × 10 = ☐

Lesson 1: **Doubles (1)**

• Find doubles

Challenge 1 Double these numbers.

a Double 1 =

b Double 2 =

c Double 3 =

d Double 5 =

Challenge 2 Draw a line to match each double to its answer.

 Double 4   Double 10   Double 6   Double 9

 Double 20   Double 8   Double 5   Double 7

(10) (16) (8) (40) (18) (12) (14) (20)

Challenge 3 Use your 100 square to find the doubles.
Write a multiplication number sentence to match.

a Double 15 = ☐   ☐ × ☐ = ☐

b Double 25 = ☐   ☐ × ☐ = ☐

c Double 50 = ☐   ☐ × ☐ = ☐

- Recognise multiples of 2, 5 and 10
- Use an array to recall 2, 5 and 10 times tables facts

Number

Challenge 1 Draw arrays to solve these multiplications.

a $5 \times 2 = \boxed{}$

b $3 \times 10 = \boxed{}$

Challenge 2 Write 2, 5 or 10 to complete each times table fact. Draw an array if you need to.

a $4 \times \boxed{} = 40$ **b** $6 \times \boxed{} = 60$ **c** $7 \times \boxed{} = 14$

d $3 \times \boxed{} = 6$ **e** $5 \times \boxed{} = 25$ **f** $2 \times \boxed{} = 10$

Challenge 3 Colour the cards that each number is a multiple of.

a 6 [2] [5] [10]

b 25 [2] [5] [10]

c 40 [2] [5] [10]

d 10 [2] [5] [10]

e 18 [2] [5] [10]

f 35 [2] [5] [10]

- Use repeated addition to multiply

Challenge 1

There are ☐ groups. There are ☐ in each group.

Add ☐ + ☐ + ☐ + ☐ = ☐

Multiply ☐ × ☐ = ☐

Challenge 2 Draw the right number of jumps to match the calculation and write the answer.

a 3 × 4 = ☐

b 5 × 2 = ☐

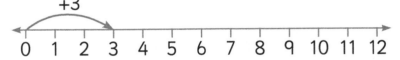

c 2 × 6 = ☐

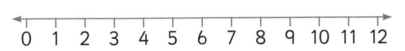

Challenge 3 Fill in the multiplication to match the addition.

a

2 + 2 + 2

☐3☐ × ☐2☐ = ☐6☐

b

3 + 3

☐ × ☐ = ☐

c

5 + 5 + 5

☐ × ☐ = ☐

d

4 + 4 + 4 + 4

☐ × ☐ = ☐

Lesson 4: **Adding groups**

- Count in groups of 2s, 5s or 10s
  to solve multiplication problems

Number

Challenge 1 Use repeated addition to solve the calculations.

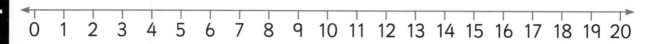

0 1 2 3 4 5 6 7 8 9 10 11 12 13 14 15 16 17 18 19 20

a $3 \times 5 =$ ☐

b $7 \times 2 =$ ☐

c $2 \times 10 =$ ☐

☐ ☐ ☐

Challenge 2 Write a multiplication for each group.

a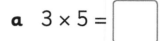

b

☐ × ☐ = ☐

☐ × ☐ = ☐

Challenge 3 Write an addition and a multiplication for each story.

a Hassan gives 5 friends 8 sweets each. How many
sweets did he give his friends altogether?

☐

b Ruksana puts her collection of shells into 6 lots
of 10. How many shells does she have altogether?

☐

Lesson 5: **Making groups**

- Make groups to solve division problems
- Use the ÷ sign

 1 How many groups of 2 are there in 6?

$6 \div 2 =$ ☐

2 How many groups of 2 are there in 10?

$10 \div 2 =$ ☐

Challenge 2 Draw dots to help answer these.

a $14 \div 2 =$ ☐

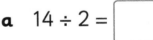

b $15 \div 5 =$ ☐

☐ ☐ ☐

c $10 \div 2 =$ ☐

d $30 \div 10 =$ ☐

Challenge 3 Draw dots in groups to help answer these.

a $24 \div 4 =$ ☐

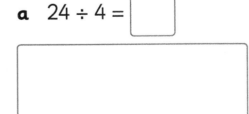

b $18 \div 3 =$ ☐

61

Lesson 6: **Dividing between 2, 5 and 10**

• Know division facts for 2, 5 and 10

Challenge 1

a How many 2s in 8?

$8 ÷ 2 =$ ☐

b How many 5s in 15?

$15 ÷ 5 =$ ☐

c How many 10s in 30?

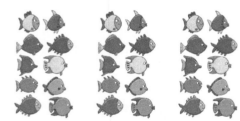

$30 ÷ 10 =$ ☐

d How many 5s in 35?

$35 ÷ 5 =$ ☐

Challenge 2 Complete these division facts.

a $16 ÷ 2 =$ ☐   **b** $10 ÷ 5 =$ ☐   **c** $45 ÷ 5 =$ ☐

d $12 ÷ 2 =$ ☐   **e** $80 ÷ 10 =$ ☐   **f** $14 ÷ 2 =$ ☐

Challenge 3 Complete the number sentences.

a $18 ÷$ ☐ $= 9$ **b** $30 ÷$ ☐ $= 6$ **c** $70 ÷$ ☐ $= 7$

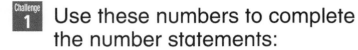
- Find division facts for 2, 5 and 10 from the 2, 5 and 10 times tables

Challenge 1 Use these numbers to complete the number statements:

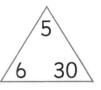

Example: 6 × ⬜ 5 = 30

a 5 × ⬜ = 30   **b** ⬜ ÷ 5 = 6   **c** 30 ÷ ⬜ = 5

Challenge 2 Write a division to match each multiplication fact.

a 4 × 2 = 8

⬜ ÷ ⬜ = ⬜

b 8 × 2 = 16

⬜ ÷ ⬜ = ⬜

c 10 × 5 = 50

⬜ ÷ ⬜ = ⬜

d 2 × 5 = 10

⬜ ÷ ⬜ = ⬜

Challenge 3 **1** Write and solve a 2, 5 or 10 times table fact.

⬜ × ⬜ = ⬜

2 Now write another multiplication and two division facts to match it.

⬜ × ⬜ = ⬜   ⬜ ÷ ⬜ = ⬜

⬜ ÷ ⬜ = ⬜

Lesson 8: **Remainders (1)**

• Share objects into two groups to discover if any are left over

Number

Challenge 1
Draw dots on the hands to share these numbers equally between 2. If there are any left over, draw the dot in the box.

a 4

b 7

Challenge 2
Draw dots in the boxes to share these numbers equally between 2. If there are any left over, draw them in the box.

a 17

b 12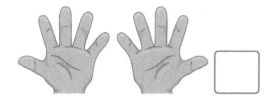

c 16

d 11

Challenge 3
Circle the numbers that will leave a remainder when shared between 2.

 10   4   7   13   8

 5   9   11   18

Lesson 1: **Doubling and halving**

• Find doubles and halves

 Challenge 1

1 Double 4 =    Now halve the answer.

2 Double 7 = Now halve the answer.

3 Double 9 = Now halve the answer.

  Challenge 2

1 Double 15 =    **2** Half of 40 =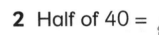

3 Double 30 = 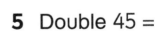   **4** Half of 20 =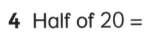

5 Double 45 =   **6** Half of 10 =

Challenge 3

1 Complete the number line.

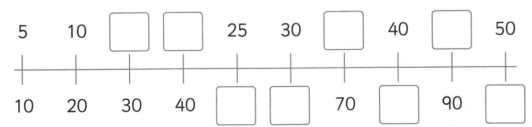

5   10   ☐   ☐   25   30   ☐   40   ☐   50

10   20   30   40   ☐   ☐   70   ☐   90   ☐

2 What do you notice about the two sets of numbers?

_____

65

- Double 2-digit numbers

You will need
- 100 square

Number

Challenge 1

Complete the word dominoes.
Write the number.

a | Double 10 | 20

b | Double 7 |

c | Double 8 |

d | Double 30 |

e | Double 20 |

f | Double 40 |

Challenge 2

Complete the word dominoes. Write the number.

a | Double 13 | 26

b | Double 42 |

c | Double 31 |

d | Double 24 |

e | Double 33 |

f | Double 44 |

g | Double 32 |

h | Double 45 |

i | Double 21 |

Challenge 3

Complete the word dominoes. Write the number.

a | Double 38 | 76

b | Double 27 |

c | Double 49 |

d | Double 47 |

e | Double 36 |

f | Double 28 |

Lesson 3: **Multiplication and division facts for 2, 5 and 10 (2)**

• Find division facts for 2, 5 and 10 from the 2, 5 and 10 times tables

 Challenge 1 Write a division fact for each multiplication.

   a $8 \times 2 = 16$ **b** $4 \times 5 = 20$

   ☐ ÷ ☐ = ☐   ☐ ÷ ☐ = ☐

Challenge 2 Write a multiplication and two divisions facts for each.

a

$6 \times 2 = 12$

☐ × ☐ = ☐

☐ ÷ ☐ = ☐

☐ ÷ ☐ = ☐

b

$8 \times 5 = 40$

☐ × ☐ = ☐

☐ ÷ ☐ = ☐

☐ ÷ ☐ = ☐

Challenge 3 Circle the division or multiplication fact that is incorrect.

$$7 \times 5 = 35$$

$$35 \div 7 = 5$$

$$7 \div 35 = 5$$

$$5 \times 7 = 35$$

$$35 \div 5 = 7$$

Lesson 4: **Multiplication and division facts for the 3× table**

Number

- Work out multiplication and division facts for the 3× table

You will need
- coloured pencil

Challenge 1 Colour the multiples of 3.

1	2	3	4	5	6	7	8	9	10
11	12	13	14	15	16	17	18	19	20
21	22	23	24	25	26	27	28	29	30

Challenge 2 Draw lines to match the facts with the multiples.

| 15 | 30 | 24 | 18 | 12 |

(4 × 3) (9 × 3) (2 × 3) (6 × 3) (3 × 3)

(7 × 3) (8 × 3) (10 × 3) (1 × 3) (5 × 3)

| 3 | 21 | 9 | 6 | 27 |

Challenge 3

1 How many 3s in 27? ☐

2 How many 3s in 9? ☐

3 18 ÷ 3 = ☐

4 21 ÷ 3 = ☐

5 How many 3s in 12? ☐

6 ☐ ÷ 3 = 10

Lesson 5: **Multiplication and division facts for the 4× table**

- Work out multiplication and division facts for the 4× table

Number

 Challenge 1 Colour the multiples of 4.

1	2	3	4	5	6	7	8	9	10
11	12	13	14	15	16	17	18	19	20
21	22	23	24	25	26	27	28	29	30
31	32	33	34	35	36	37	38	39	40

Challenge 2 Draw lines to match the facts with the multiples.

12	32	16	28	8

(4 × 4) (9 × 4) (2 × 4) (6 × 4) (3 × 4)

(7 × 4) (8 × 4) (10 × 4) (1 × 4) (5 × 4)

36	20	24	40	4

Challenge 3

1 $32 \div 4 =$ ☐

2 How many 4s in 28? ☐

3 $40 \div 4 =$ ☐

4 How many 4s in 24? ☐

5 $16 \div 4 =$ ☐

6 How many 4s in 44? ☐

Lesson 6: **Remainders (2)**

• Solve a division and say how many are left over

Challenge 1

Draw dots on the hands. If there are any left over, draw the dots in the box.

a $8 \div 2$

b $11 \div 2$

c $16 \div 5$

d $4 \div 2$

Challenge 2

Draw dots on the hands. If there are any left over, draw the dots in the box. Write the answer including the remainder.

a $9 \div 2 =$ ⬚

b $14 \div 2 =$ ⬚

c $19 \div 2 =$ ⬚

d $18 \div 5 =$ ⬚

Challenge 3

Draw dots on the hands. If there are any left over, draw the dots in the box. Write the answer including the remainder.

a $11 \div 3 =$ ⬚

b $27 \div 4 =$ ⬚

c $16 \div 3 =$ ⬚

d $15 \div 4 =$ ⬚

Lesson 7: **Multiplication and division problems (1)**

• Solve multiplication and division problems

 1 1 3 brothers have 5 toy cars each. How many cars altogether? ☐

2 2 cats shared 6 fish. How many fish did they have each? ☐

 2 1 Hassan wants to pick enough plums for his 3 sisters to have 4 each. How many must he pick? ☐

2 Holly shared 15 seeds between 3 pots. How many did she plant in each pot? ☐

3 There are 5 learners on a table at school. The teacher handed out 30 crayons to share. How many crayons can they have each? ☐

 3 1 There are 15 learners in my sister's class. There is double that number in my class. How many learners are in my class? ☐

2 Ingrid found 18 seashells and shared them between 4 friends. How many did each friend get? ☐

How many seashells were left over? ☐

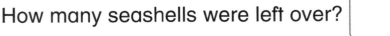

Lesson 8: **Multiplication and division problems (2)**

Number

• Solve multiplication and division problems

Challenge 1 A cake is cut into 10 pieces and shared between 5 people. How many pieces does each person get?

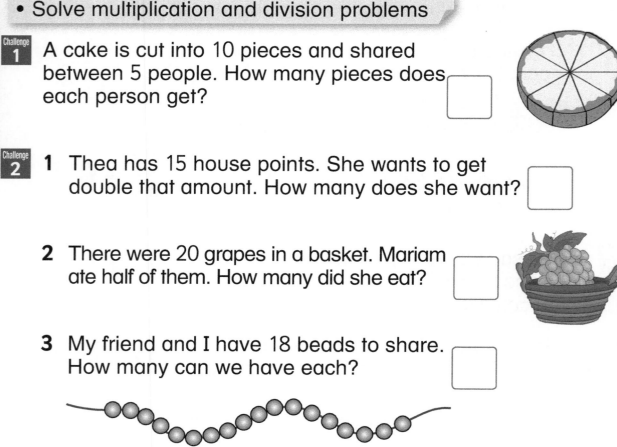

Challenge 2

1 Thea has 15 house points. She wants to get double that amount. How many does she want?

2 There were 20 grapes in a basket. Mariam ate half of them. How many did she eat?

3 My friend and I have 18 beads to share. How many can we have each?

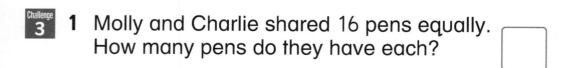

Challenge 3

1 Molly and Charlie shared 16 pens equally. How many pens do they have each?

2 60 balloons are shared between 29 people. How many balloons does each person get?

How many balloons are left over?

Lesson 1: **Recognising and naming 2D shapes**

- Recognise and name circles, triangles, squares, rectangles, pentagons and hexagons

You will need
- coloured pencil

Challenge 1 Colour the matching 2D shape in each row.

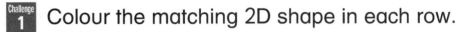
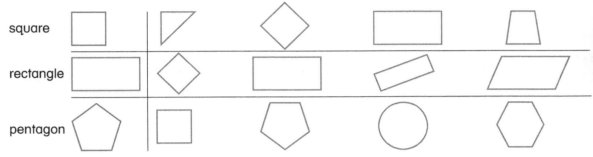

square

rectangle

pentagon

Challenge 2

1 Colour the pentagons and hexagons to find your way home.

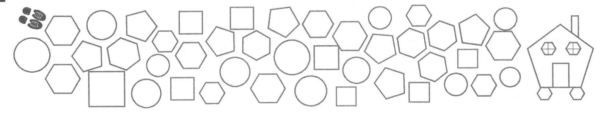

2 Draw lines to match the same shapes.

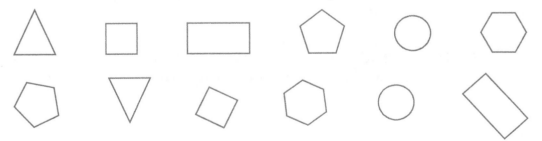

Challenge 3 Draw a line to match each 2D shape to its name.

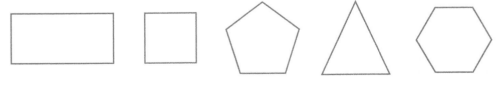

hexagon   square   rectangle   pentagon

Lesson 2: **Describing 2D shapes**

Geometry

• Describe 2D shapes by talking about the sides and corners

Challenge 1

Colour the shapes with 4 sides red.
Colour the shape with 5 sides blue.

Challenge 2

1 Colour the shapes that have all sides the same length.

2 Colour the shape with two long and two short sides.

Challenge 3

Complete the table.

2D shape	Number of straight sides	Number of curved sides	Number of corners
☐	4	0	4
▭			
○			
⬠			
⬡			
△			

74

Lesson 3: **Visualising and drawing 2D shapes**

• Imagine a 2D shape and draw it

You will need
- geoboard
- elastic bands
- ruler

Challenge 1 Use the geoboard to make a rectangle and a triangle.
Then draw your shapes below.

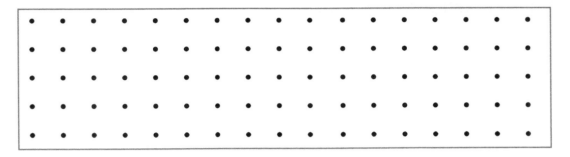

Challenge 2 Use the geoboard to make a square and two different triangles. Then draw your shapes below.

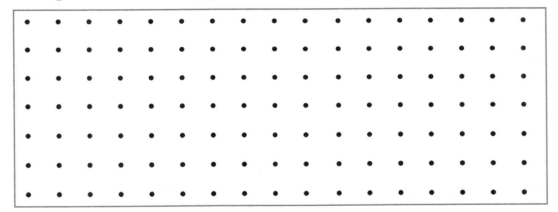

Challenge 3 Use the geoboard to make a pentagon and a hexagon. Then draw your shapes below.

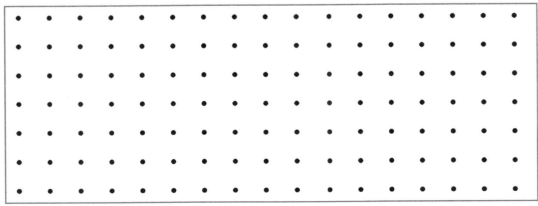

Lesson 4: **Sorting 2D shapes**

• Compare and sort 2D shapes

Use these shapes for Challenges 1–3.

A B C D E F G H

Challenge 1 Write the letter of the shapes in the correct pot.

hexagon   not a hexagon

Challenge 2 Write the letter of the shapes in the correct column in the table.

Regular shape	Irregular shape

Challenge 3 Sort the shapes by writing the letters in the correct box.

4 or fewer straight sides	5 or more sides	Straight sides

76

Lesson 1: **Recognising and naming 3D shapes**

- Recognise and name spheres, cones, cylinders, cubes, cuboids and pyramids

You will need
- red and blue coloured pencils

 Challenge 1 Shade the 2D shapes red and the 3D shapes blue.

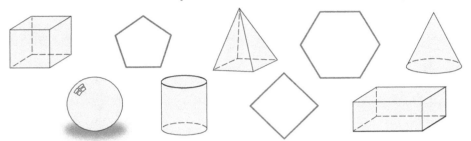

Challenge 2 Match each object to its shape.

Challenge 3 Circle the correct 3D shape name for each row.

	triangle	hexagon	pyramid	cone
	sphere	cone	cylinder	circle
	pentagon	cube	rectangle	square
	cone	sphere	triangle	cuboid
	hexagon	cube	circle	cuboid

Lesson 2: **Describing 3D shapes**

- Talk about the faces, corners and edges of 3D shapes

You will need
- red and blue coloured pencil

 Challenge 1

Trace over each edge in red.
Place a blue dot in each corner.

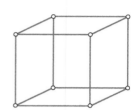 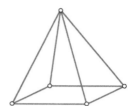

Challenge 2

A    B   C   D

Complete the table.

	Name of shape	Number of faces	Number of corners	Number of edges
A				
B				
C				
D				

Challenge 3 Circle the 3D shape.

Which shape am I? I have 3 faces, 2 edges and no corners.

Lesson 3: **Making 3D shapes**

• Make 3D shapes

You will need
- straws
- modelling clay
- paper
- scissors
- glue

Work with a partner.

Challenge 1 Use straws and modelling clay to make a cuboid. Draw your cuboid.

Challenge 2 Use straws and modelling clay to make a pyramid. Draw your pyramid.

Challenge 3 Use paper to make a cylinder. Draw your cylinder.

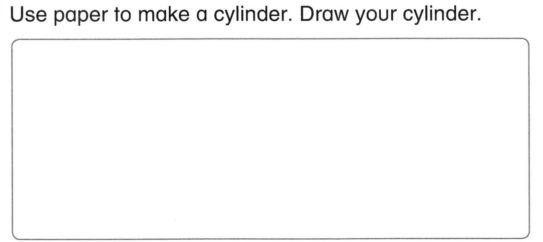

Geometry

Lesson 4: **Sorting 3D shapes**

Geometry

• Compare and sort 3D shapes

You will need

• red, blue and green coloured pencil

Challenge 1

Colour red all the shapes with 3 or fewer faces.

Colour blue all the shapes with 4 or more faces.

    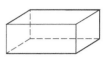

Challenge 2

1 Colour red all the shapes with less than 8 edges.
Colour blue all the shapes with 8 or more edges.

   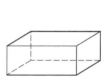

2 Colour red all the shapes with less than 5 corners.
Colour blue all the shapes with 5 or more corners.

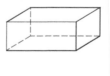

Challenge 3

Colour the shapes that fit each sorting rule.

Curved faces only

Flat faces only

Curved and flat faces

• Recognise symmetry in patterns

Challenge 1 Complete the patterns to make them symmetrical.

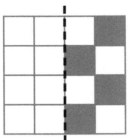 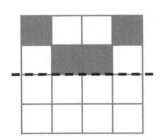

Challenge 2 Complete the patterns to make them symmetrical.

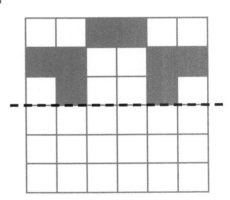 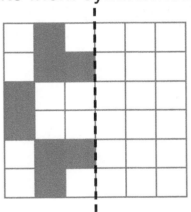

Challenge 3 Complete the picture of the robot.

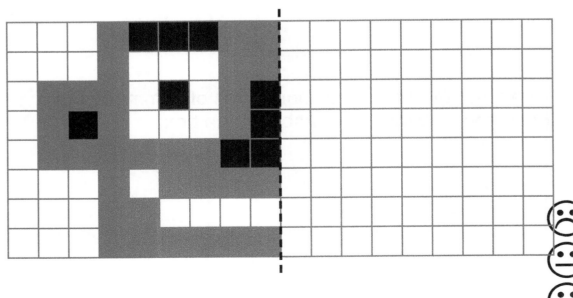

Geometry

Lesson 2: **Symmetry in 2D shapes**

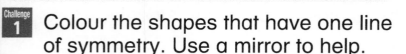

• Recognise symmetry in 2D shapes

You will need
• coloured pencils

Challenge 1

Colour the shapes that have one line of symmetry. Use a mirror to help.

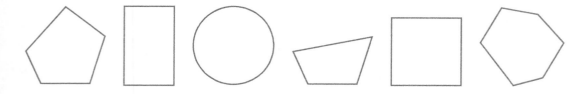

Challenge 2

Colour the shapes that have both vertical and horizontal lines of symmetry. Use a mirror to help.

h o r i z o n t a l

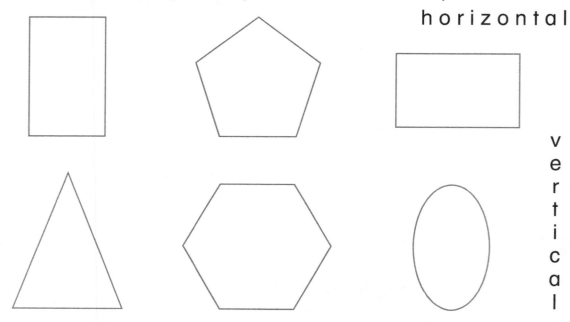

v
e
r
t
i
c
a
l

Challenge 3

Use a mirror to find how many lines of symmetry there are in each shape. Write the number in the box.

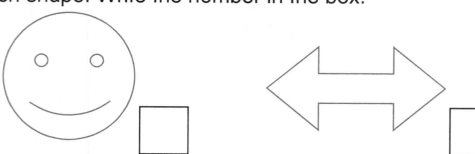

Geometry

Lesson 3: **Drawing lines of symmetry**

- Draw horizontal and vertical lines of symmetry

You will need
- mirror
- ruler

Challenge 1 Draw the line of symmetry for each shape. Check with a mirror.

a
b

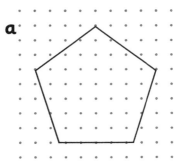
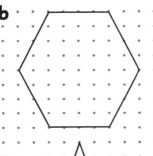

Challenge 2 Draw two lines of symmetry for each shape. Check with a mirror.

a
b

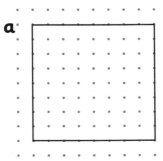
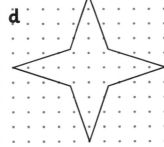

c
d

Challenge 3 Draw the lines of symmetry.

a
b
c

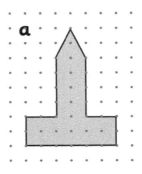
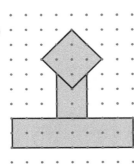
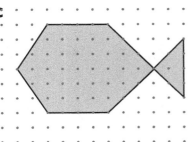

83

Lesson 4: **Symmetry all around us**

• Recognise when an everyday object has one or more lines of symmetry

You will need
• coloured pencils

Challenge 1 Circle the objects that show symmetry.

a 　　b 　　c 　　d

Challenge 2 Draw the line of symmetry on each picture.

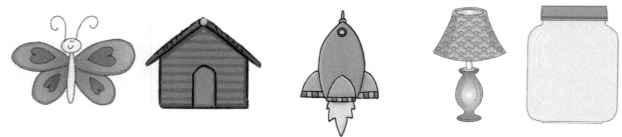

Challenge 3 Use four different colours to shade any 12 shapes on one side of the line of symmetry, then colour 12 shapes on the other side of the symmetry so that the rug is symmetrical.

Lesson 1: **Position**

- Follow and give instructions for position

Challenge 1 Circle the correct position of Ted.

a  b  c

next to	behind	on top
between	in front	under

Challenge 2 Complete the sentences using the key words.

above	next to	in front of

The cows are _____ the trees.

The calf stands _____ its mum.

The sun is _____ the trees.

Challenge 3 Draw each creature to show its position in the picture.

On top of the mushroom is a

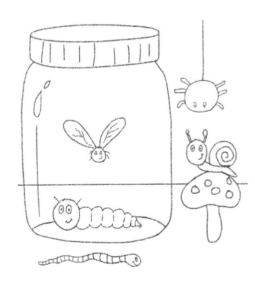

Hanging next to the jar is a

In front of the jar is a

85

Geometry

- Follow and give directions to move from one position to another

You will need
- blue and red coloured pencils

Challenge 1

Draw lines to match the directions to the arrows.

forward   left   right

Challenge 2

Colour blue the things facing right. Colour red the things facing left.

Challenge 3

Help the cat get to the milk by giving it directions. Use the code below. The first 2 have been done for you.

Forward = F
Right = R
Left = L

1 _____ F 3 _____   2 __ Face R, then F2. __

3 _____   4 _____

5 _____   6 _____

7 _____   8 _____

9 _____

86

Lesson 3: **Whole, half and quarter turns**

- Make whole, half and quarter turns clockwise and anticlockwise

You will need
- coloured pencils

Challenge 1 Draw lines to match the directions to the circles.

clockwise   anticlockwise

Challenge 2 Mark the direction on each circle.

a half turn
clockwise

a quarter turn
anticlockwise

a whole turn
clockwise

a whole turn
anticlockwise

a half turn
anticlockwise

a quarter turn
clockwise

Challenge 3 Draw the objects on the tables.

If the girl makes $\frac{1}{4}$ of a turn clockwise she faces the crayons

If the girl makes a whole turn she faces the plants

If the girl makes $\frac{1}{4}$ of a turn anticlockwise
she faces the paints and brushes

Lesson 4: **Right angles**

Unit 14

• Recognise a quarter turn is a right angle

You will need

• red, blue and green coloured pencils

Challenge 1 Colour the arrows that are right angles.

Challenge 2 For each object, draw a small red square at every right angle.

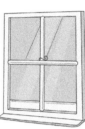

Challenge 3 For each shape:
- draw a small red square at every right angle
- draw a small blue circle at every angle larger than a right angle
- draw a small green circle at every angle smaller than a right angle.

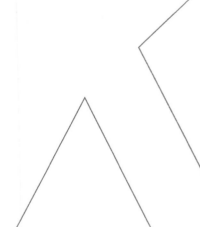
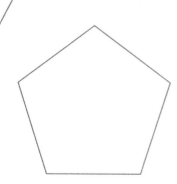

Geometry

88

Lesson 1: **Recognising all coins and notes**

- Recognise all coins up to 50c and notes up to $50

Challenge 1 Draw lines to match the front and back of the notes.

Challenge 2 Write the value of each coin and note.

	$20		$2

Challenge 3 Write the name of each coin and note.

Lesson 2: **Finding totals (1)**

- Find totals up to 50c and $20

Measure

Challenge 1 Total the coins.

a   **10**   +   **5**   +   **5**   = [ ] cents

b   **10**   +   **5**   +   **1**   = [ ] cents

c   **10**   +   **1**   +   **1**   = [ ] cents

d   **10**   +   **10**   +   **5**   = [ ] cents

Challenge 2 Find the total of each purse.

a
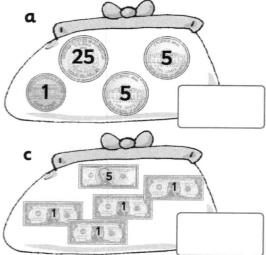

b

c

d
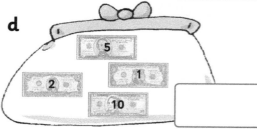

Challenge 3 Draw two different ways of making the same value.

a   **50**

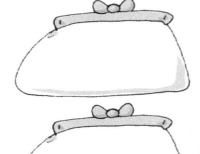

b   **20**

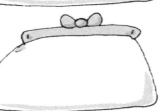

Lesson 3: **Finding totals to pay an amount (1)**

- Make totals up to 50c and $20 to pay an exact amount

You will need
- coloured pencils

Challenge 1 What is the total cost of the bike and helmet?

$11

$4

Challenge 2

1 An ice lolly costs 45c. Colour the coins to make the amount.

10 5

25 10 5

2 A cinema visit costs $15. Draw a combination of notes that totals $15.

Challenge 3 Is there enough money to buy each item? Circle yes or no.

$15	10	1	1	1	yes no
$4	5				yes no
$13	10	5			yes no

Lesson 4: **Finding totals and working out change (1)**

• Find totals and give change

Challenge 1

Work out the totals. Use coins if you need to.

a 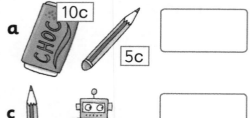 10c 5c

b  50c $2

c  5c 50c

d  10c $2

Challenge 2

1 Work out the change from 25c **25**. Use coins if you need to.

a 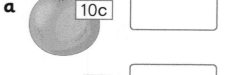 10c

b 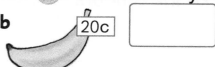 20c

c 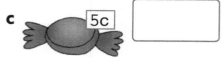 5c

d 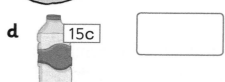 15c

2 Work out the change from $10. **10**. Use notes if you need to.

a  $2

b  $4

c  $5

d $8

Challenge 3

Look at the items in Challenge 1. Work out the totals. Then work out the change from $5. Use coins if you need to.

a

b

Total = ___   Total = ___

Change from $5 = ___   Change from $5 = ___

92

Lesson 1: **Finding totals (2)**

• Recognise all coins and notes and find totals

Challenge 1

Find the totals.

a (10) (10) (10) (10) ☐

b (5) (5) (5) ☐

c [2] [2] [2] [2] ☐

d [10] [10] [10] ☐

Challenge 2

Find the totals.

a (25) (10) (10) (5) ☐

b (10) (10) (10) (5) (5) ☐

c [20] [10] [10] [2] ☐

d [10] [5] [5] [2] [1] ☐

Challenge 3

Use doubles to find the totals.

a (25) (25) (10) (10) ☐

b (50) (50) ☐

c [10] [10] [2] [2] ☐

d [10] [5] [10] [5] ☐

Measure

93

Lesson 2: **Finding totals to pay an amount (2)**

• Find totals in coins and notes to pay an exact amount

You will need
• coloured pencils

Challenge 1

Colour the coins you could use to pay for each item.

a 80c — 10 5 10 50 25 10

b 75c — 10 5 10 50 25 10

Challenge 2

1 Colour the coins you could use to pay for each item.

a 64c — 10 5 1 50 1 10 1 1

b 95c — 10 5 10 50 25 5 5

2 Colour the notes you could use to pay for each item.

a $16 — 5 1 10 1 2

b $7 — 10 1 2 2 5 2

Challenge 3

Colour the notes and coins you could use to pay for the beach chair.

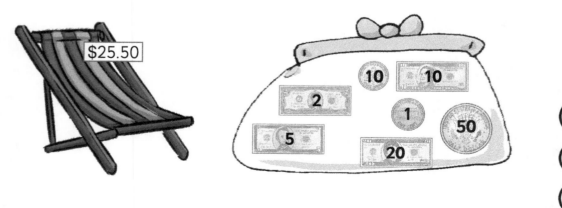

$25.50 — 10 10 2 1 50 5 20

Lesson 3: **Finding totals and working out change (2)**

- Find totals in coins and notes up to $50 and work out change

You will need
- real or toy money

Measure

Challenge 1 Work out the totals.

 $13 $18 $28  $7.50

a  ____

b ____

c  ____

Challenge 2 **1** Work out the change from $20.

a  $8.20 ____

b 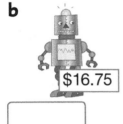 $16.75 ____

c  $4.60 ____

d  $10.50 ____

2 Work out the change from $40.

a  $17 ____

b  $29.50 ____

c  $36.75 ____

Challenge 3 Look at the clothes at the top of the page. Work out the totals and the change from $50.

a  ____ ____

b ____ ____

c ____ ____

Lesson 4: **Finding totals and working out change (3)**

- Find totals and work out change for two-step money word problems

You will need
- real or toy money

Challenge 1

Work out the totals and the change given from $10.

$4 $3.50 $2 $1.50 $1.20

a Jon bought , and .   Total ☐ Change ☐

b Amira bought and   Total ☐ Change ☐

c Hanneke bought   Total ☐ Change ☐

Challenge 2

Work out the totals and answer the questions.

$16 $22 $18 $7.90 $4.99 $4.60

a Hana has $15, she wants to buy a . She needs ☐.

b Bobby has $50, he wants to buy a and 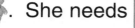.
How much change will he be given? ☐

c Sophie has $10. She buys .
How much change does she get? ☐

Challenge 3

$4 $4.50 $3.75 $5.20

a Dora has $4.85. How much more does she need to
go on the 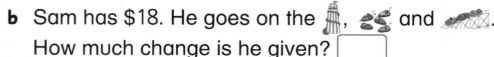. ☐

b Sam has $18. He goes on the .
How much change is he given? ☐

Lesson 1: **Measuring lengths and choosing non-standard units**

> • Estimate and measure length with units of measure that are the same

> **You will need**
> • interlocking cubes
> • paper clips

Challenge 1 How many cubes does each dinosaur bone measure?

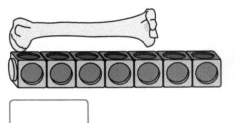 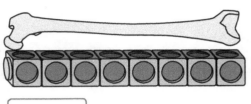

[ ]   [ ]

Challenge 2 Estimate the length of each pencil in paper clips. Then use paper clips to measure each pencil.

a

Estimate: [ ]   Length: [ ]

b

Estimate: [ ]   Length: [ ]

c

Estimate: [ ]   Length: [ ]

d

Estimate: [ ]   Length: [ ]

Challenge 3

1 Estimate the length of each pencil in Challenge 2 in cubes. Then use cubes to measure each pencil.

a Estimate: [ ]   Length: [ ]   b Estimate: [ ]   Length: [ ]

c Estimate: [ ]   Length: [ ]   d Estimate: [ ]   Length: [ ]

2 Which is best to measure the lengths of the pencil: paper clips or cubes? _____

Why? _____

97

Lesson 2: **Standard units: metre, centimetre**

• Recognise and use the standard units: metre and centimetre

Challenge 1

Tick the things that are longer than a 30 cm ruler.
Circle the things that are shorter than a 30 cm ruler.

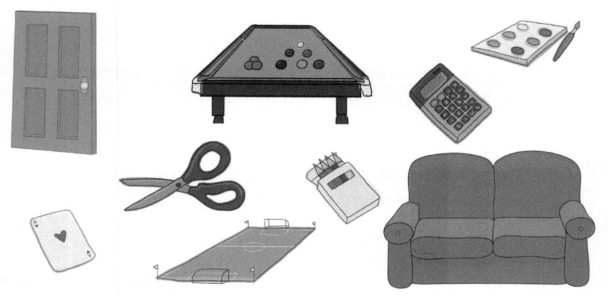

Challenge 2

Draw one example in each box.

Shorter than 30 cm	Longer than 30 cm	Longer than 1 m

Challenge 3

Shade a 1 cm length on the ruler and fill in the missing numbers.

12

Lesson 3: **Choosing suitable standard units: length**

• Estimate and measure length in centimetres and metres, choosing the best unit and instrument

You will need
• ruler

 Challenge 1

1 Estimate your hand span.  ☐ cm

2 Use a ruler to measure your hand span in centimetres. ☐ cm

Challenge 2 Estimate the length of each object, then use a ruler to measure each object in centimetres.

Object	Estimate	Measure
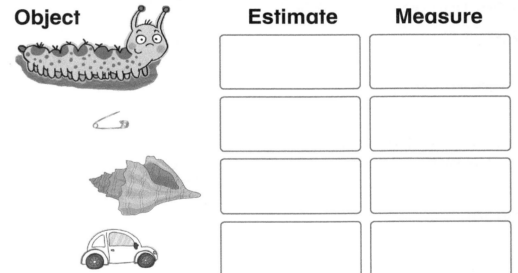		

Challenge 3 Circle the best estimate for each object.

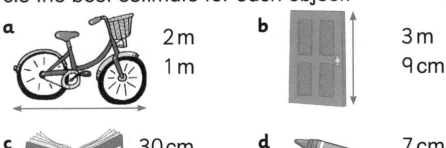

a    2 m   1 m

b   3 m   9 cm

c    30 cm   10 cm

d   7 cm   1 cm

Lesson 4: **Comparing lengths**

Measure

• Use a ruler to compare lengths

You will need
• ruler

Challenge 1

Use a ruler to measure each object.
Circle the longer object in each pair.

a

b

Challenge 2

1 Use a ruler to measure
the pencil. Then draw a
longer and a shorter pencil.

longer

shorter

2 Use a ruler to measure the belt. Then draw a longer and a
shorter belt.

longer

shorter

Challenge 3

Measure each belt then write 'longer' or 'shorter to compare them.

A

B

C

Belt A _____ cm   Belt B _____ cm   Belt C _____ cm

Belt A is _____ than Belt B. Belt B is _____ than Belt C.

Belt A is _____ than Belt C.

100

Lesson 1: **Measuring weights and choosing non-standard units**

- Estimate and measure weights with units of measure that are the same

You will need
- balance scale
- two objects to weigh
- pile of smaller items used for weighing, such as cubes

Measure

Challenge 1 Circle the lighter object on each balance scale.

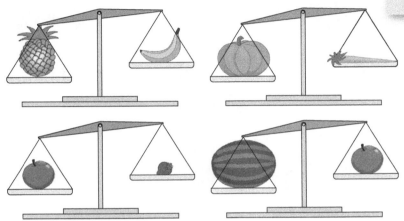

Challenge 2 Weigh two different objects. Use the balance scales to show what you did. Estimate the weight of each object first.

Estimate: [ ]   Estimate: [ ]

Challenge 3 Draw the items needed to make each scale balance.

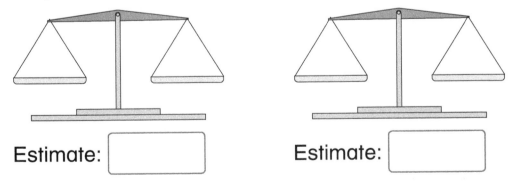

= 5 cubes   = 2 crayons

a

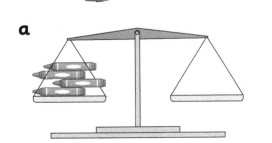

b

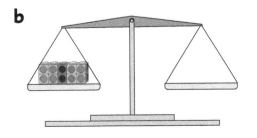

😦
😐
☺

101

Lesson 2: **Standard units: kilogram and gram**

• Recognise and use the standard units: kilogram and gram

Measure

Challenge 1 Circle the objects heavier than a kilogram.

Challenge 2 Circle the measurement you would use for each object.

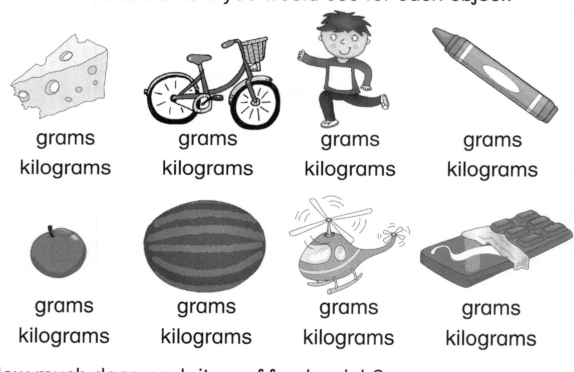

| grams | grams | grams | grams |
| kilograms | kilograms | kilograms | kilograms |

| grams | grams | grams | grams |
| kilograms | kilograms | kilograms | kilograms |

Challenge 3 How much does each item of food weigh?

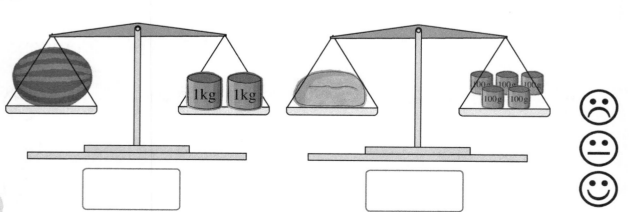

Lesson 3: **Choosing suitable standard units: weight**

- Estimate and weigh in kilograms and grams, choosing the best unit

You will need
- balance scale
- two objects to weigh
- 1 kg, 500 g, 200 g and 100 g weights

Challenge 1 How many grams is each burger?

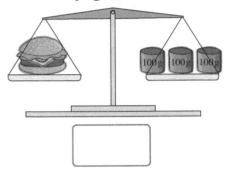

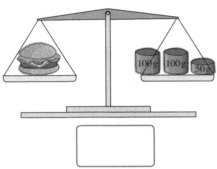

Challenge 2 Use weights to weigh two different objects. Use the balance scales to show what you did. Estimate the weight of each object first.

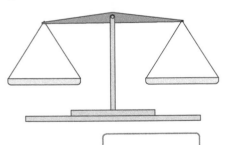

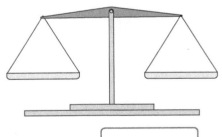

Estimate: [   ]

Estimate: [   ]

Challenge 3 Match the object to its weight.

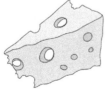

100 g

400 g

1 kg

6 kg

103

Lesson 4: **Comparing weights**

* Compare weights in kilograms and grams

Challenge 1
Write the weight of each plate of cakes. Then complete the sentences.

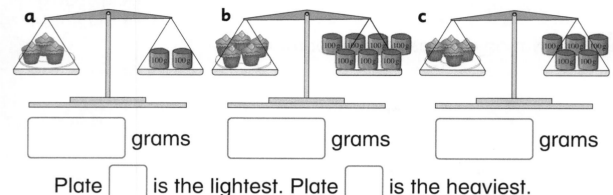

a [ ] **grams**   b [ ] **grams**   c [ ] **grams**

Plate [ ] is the lightest. Plate [ ] is the heaviest.

Challenge 2
Write the weight of each box of food. Then complete the sentences.

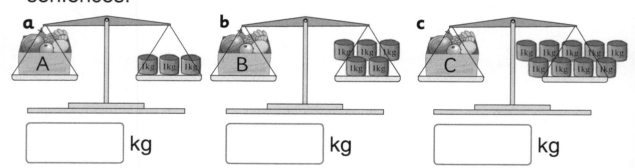

a [ ] **kg**   b [ ] **kg**   c [ ] **kg**

Box C is [ ] kg heavier than Box A.

Challenge 3
Write the weight of each box of food. Then complete the sentence.

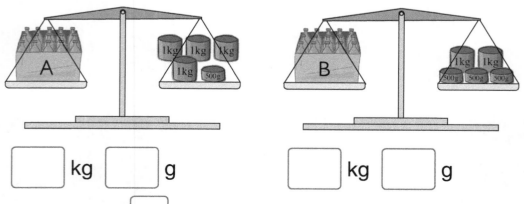

[ ] kg [ ] g   [ ] kg [ ] g

Box A is [ ] kg heavier than Box B.

104

Lesson 1: **Measuring capacities using non-standard units**

- Estimate and measure capacity using units of measure that are the same

You will need
- containers of different sizes
- water
- coloured pencils

Challenge 1 Circle the correct terms.

a Holds more than/less than a

b Holds more than/less than a

c Holds more than/less than a

Challenge 2 Take an egg cup and a jug. Draw them below. Estimate how many egg cups of water the jug will hold. Then find out.

Jug	Egg cup

estimate ☐   actual ☐

Challenge 3 What is the capacity of one small bottle in tablespoons?

 holds the same as   holds the same as ☐ tablespoons

105

Lesson 2: **The litre (l)**

- Recognise more than, less than and a whole litre on a measuring instrument

Measure

Challenge 1

Circle the containers that hold less than 1 litre.

Tick the containers that hold more than 1 litre.

Challenge 2

1 Colour each container to show 1 litre.

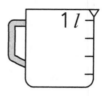  

2 Colour each container to show less than 1 litre.

 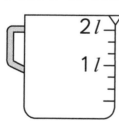 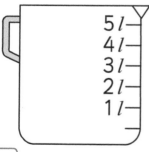

Challenge 3

How many litres of water altogether? ☐ litres

Lesson 3: **Measuring capacities using standard units**

- Estimate and measure capacity in litres

You will need
- containers of different sizes
- 1 litre measuring jug
- water
- coloured pencils

Challenge 1

Look at your containers. Draw them below to show how much water you think each one holds.

I think these containers will hold **less than 1 litre.**	I think these containers will hold **1 litre.**	I think these containers will hold **more than 1 litre.**

Challenge 2

Look at your containers. Draw them below to show how much water each one holds.

Holds **less than 1 litre.**	Holds about **1 litre.**	Holds **more than 1 litre.**

Challenge 3

Look at the containers that hold more than 1 litre.
How many litres does each of these containers hold?

Lesson 4: **Comparing capacities using standard units**

Measure

• Use litres to compare capacities

Challenge 1

Circle the container with the greatest capacity.

Tick the container with the smallest capacity.

2 *l*   3 *l*   1 *l*

Challenge 2

Write the capacity of each of the containers in the boxes. Then for each pair of containers, write the less than (<) or greater than (>) sign in the circle.

a
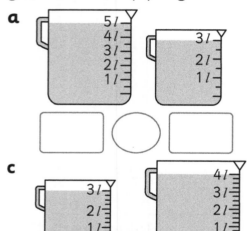

b
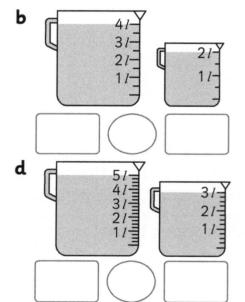

c

d

Challenge 3

Circle the combination with the largest capacity.

a
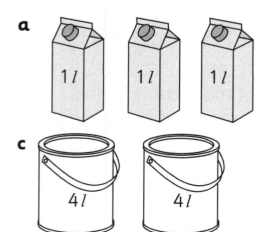
1 *l*   1 *l*   1 *l*

b

2 *l*   2 *l*   2 *l*   2 *l*   2 *l*

c
4 *l*   4 *l*

d

3 *l*   3 *l*

108

Lesson 1: **The units of time**

- Know different units of time
  and order the months by name

You will need
- red and blue pencil

Challenge 1 Underline the month it is now in red. Underline the first
month of the year in blue. Circle the last month of the year.

January   February   March   April   May   June   July   August
September   October   November   December   September

Challenge 2 **1** Which month comes next?

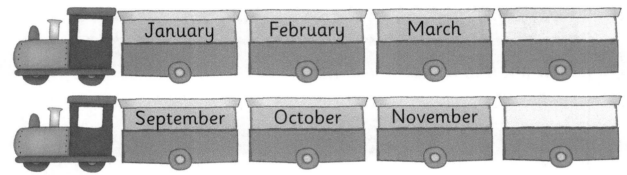

January   February   March   ____

September   October   November   ____

2 Write in the missing numbers.

a 1 year = ☐ months = ☐ weeks

b 1 week = ☐ days

c 1 day = ☐ hours

d 1 hour = ☐ minutes

e 1 minute = ☐ seconds

Challenge 3 Complete the table.

One month before	Month	One month later
	May	
	July	
	August	

Lesson 2: **Reading the time to the half hour**

- Read half past the hour in digital numbers and on a clock face

 Challenge 1 Circle the digital time that matches the clock face.

a

b

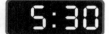 

Challenge 2 Draw lines to match the times.

Challenge 3 Circle the clock face that shows one hour later than each digital clock.

a

b

Lesson 3: **Showing the time to the half hour**

• Write half past in digital time, and mark the hands on a clock

 Challenge 1 Read each clock and write it in digital time.

a    **b**    **c**    **d**

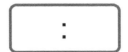   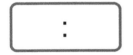   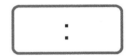   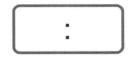

 Challenge 2 **1** Read the time and write it in digital time.

a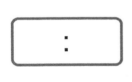

b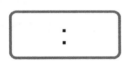

2 Read the time and mark it on the clock face.

a

b

 Challenge 3 Read the time and show what the time was 1 hour earlier.

a

b

Measure

Lesson 4: **Measuring time**

• Use familiar words to measure time

Challenge 1 Circle how long each activity would take.

seconds

minutes hours

seconds

minutes hours

seconds

minutes hours

seconds

minutes hours

seconds

minutes hours

seconds

minutes hours

Challenge 2

1 Circle how long it takes to:

brush your hair
1 second

1 minute 1 hour

blink
1 second

1 minute 1 hour

watch a movie
1 second

1 minute 1 hour

2 Draw something that takes more than an hour.

Challenge 3 Join the matching times.

sixty seconds   half an hour

30 minutes   15 minutes

quarter of an hour   one minute

120 seconds   1 year

12 months   2 minutes

Lesson 1: **Data in lists and tables**

- Collect, record and read information in lists and tables

Challenge 1 Complete the shopping list using the table.

Fruit	Total
banana	5
melon	2
orange	4

Shopping list

☐ bananas

☐ melons

☐ oranges

Challenge 2 Sort the pets into the table. How many are there?

Pet	Total
🐟	
🐱	
🦜	

Challenge 3 Sort the shapes into the table. How many are there?

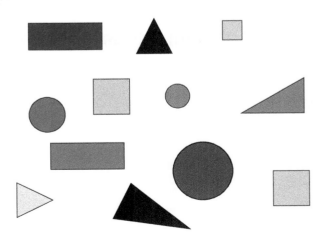

Shape	Total
◻	
▲	
▬	
●	

Handling data

113

Lesson 2: **Carroll and Venn diagrams with one sorting rule**

• Read and create Carroll and Venn diagrams with one sorting rule

Challenge 1

Sort the pictures. Draw them in the Venn diagram.

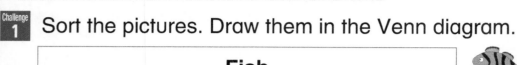

Fish

fish with stripes

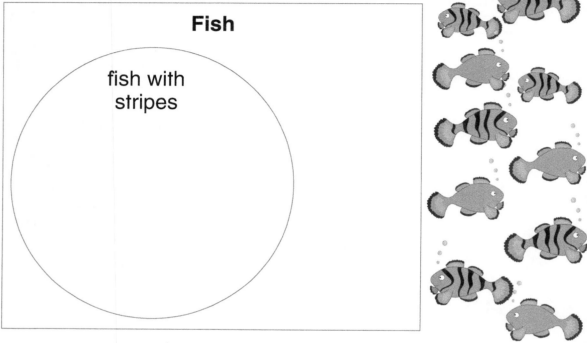

Challenge 2

1 Sort the pictures and draw them in the correct place on the Carroll diagram.

straight edges	no straight edges

2 Complete the Venn diagram.

Numbers to 10

odd

Challenge 3

1 Write three names that begin with the letter M in the Carroll diagram.

2 Write three names that begin with the letter M in the Venn diagram.

3 Write two more names in each diagram that do not begin with M.

First names

beginning with M

First names

beginning with M	not beginning with M

115

Lesson 3: **Carroll diagrams with two sorting rules**

• Read and create Carroll diagrams with two sorting rules

Challenge 1 Draw one example in each box that fits the sorting rules.

Flowers

	yellow	blue
5 petals		
3 petals		

Challenge 2

1 Find out the ages of eight learners in your class and write their names in the Carroll diagram.

Title: _____

	aged 7	not aged 7
is a boy		
is a girl		

2 Look at the Carroll diagram and answer the questions.

	can ride a bike	cannot ride a bike
can swim	Rani, Mariam	Molly, Jess, Amira
cannot swim	Lily, Lin, Ife	Daima, Emmy

a Can Ife ride a bike?

b How many girls can ride a bike, but cannot swim?

c Which girls can ride a bike and swim?

_____

_____

d How many girls can swim?

 Challenge 3

1 Write some headings to make this Carroll diagram true.

2 Draw a shape that follows the rules in the empty box.

Title: _____

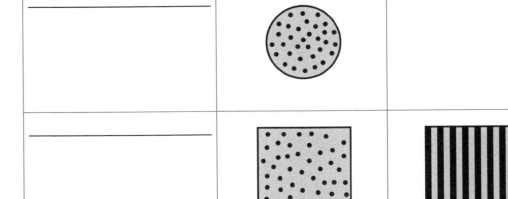

Lesson 4: **Venn diagrams with two sorting rules**

• Read and create Venn diagrams with two sorting rules

Challenge 1

Draw two examples in each part of the Venn diagram.

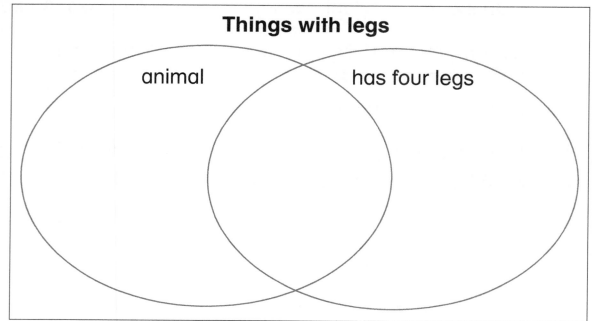

Things with legs

animal   has four legs

Challenge 2

1 Work out the two sorting rules then write the labels.

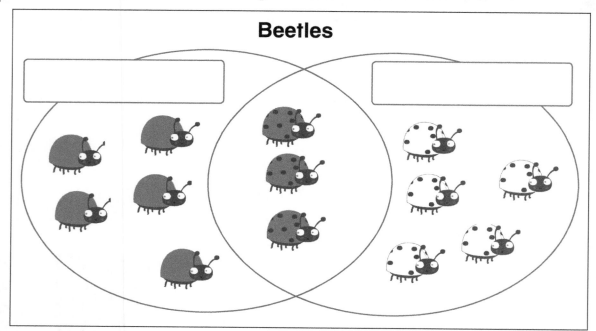

Beetles

Handling data

2 Write the numbers into the Venn diagram.

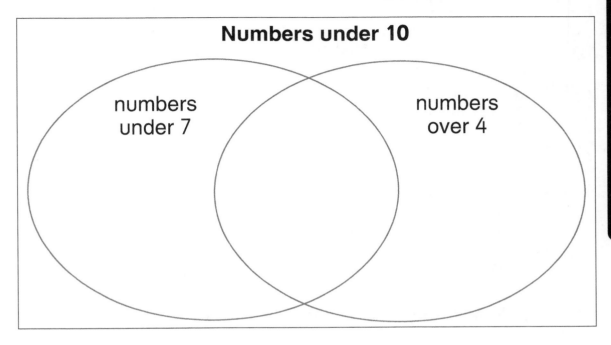

Numbers under 10

numbers under 7

numbers over 4

Challenge 3 Question eight people in your class and write their names in the Venn diagram. Give the diagram a title.

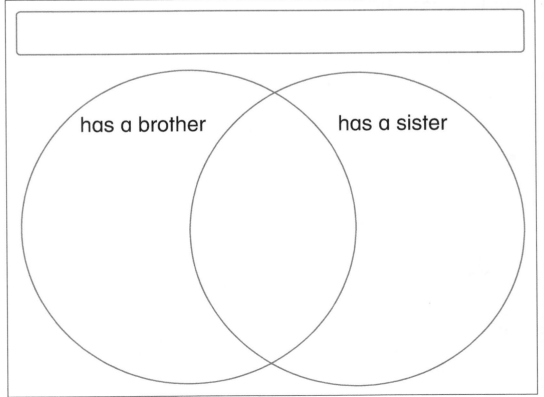

has a brother

has a sister

119

Lesson 5: **Block graphs**

- Collect, record and read information on a block graph

You will need
- coloured pencils

Challenge 1

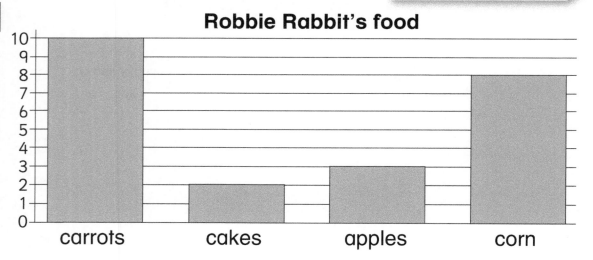

Robbie Rabbit's food

carrots   cakes   apples   corn

a How many apples did Robbie eat?

b What is Robbie's favourite food? _____

Represent the information in a block graph. Use a different colour for each shape.

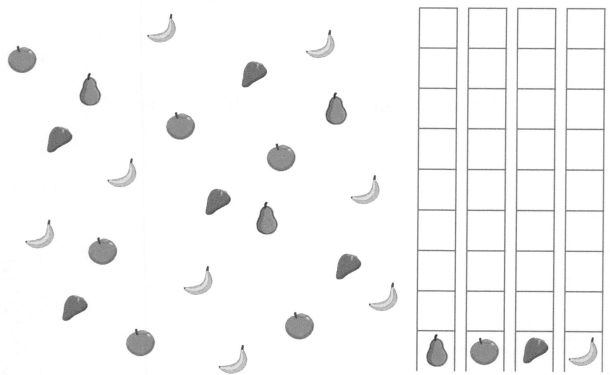

120

Challenge 3

Represent the information in a block graph. Use a different colour for each type of transport.

🚲	6
🚗	4
👟	5
🚌	8

Lesson 6: **Pictograms**

- Collect, record and read information on a pictogram

You will need
- coloured pencils

Challenge 1

Draw a pictogram for the number of animals in the zoo.

Animals in the zoo

elephants	2
tigers	4
monkeys	8

Animals in the zoo

_____									
_____									
_____									

Challenge 2

Draw a pictogram for the number of milkshakes sold.

Milkshakes sold

Milkshake	Number
banana	9
strawberry	2
chocolate	5
mango	10

Milkshakes sold

_____									
_____									
_____									
_____									

Challenge 3

Favourite sports

cycling

basketball

tennis

swimming

a How many people like cycling?

b How many more people like basketball than tennis?

c How many people were surveyed altogether?

d What is the most popular activity?

_____

e Write the activities in order from least to most popular.

_____

_____

_____

_____

Handling data

Handling data

• Ask a question and conduct a survey, showing results in a graph

You will need
• coloured pencils

Challenge 1 Draw a block graph.

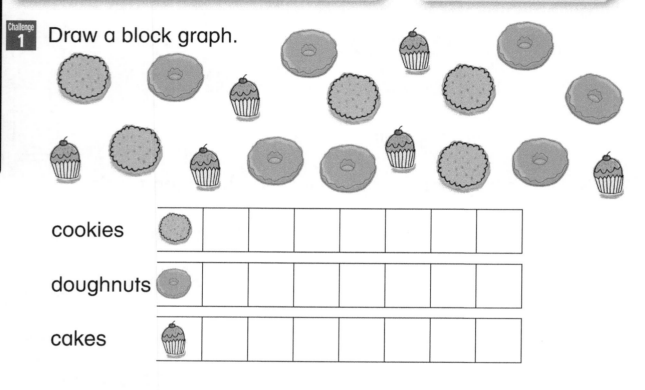

cookies								

doughnuts								

cakes								

The most popular snack is _____.

Challenge 2

1 Collect some data from your class.

Which pet would you like to own?

Pet	Total
cat	
fish	
bird	
horse	

Handling data

2 Make a block diagram with your results

Challenge 3

As a class, carry out a survey of favourite colours. Make a tally chart. Show your results in a block graph. Include a title and colour names.

Colour	Total

125

Lesson 8: **Collecting, recording and interpreting data (2)**

Handling data

• Ask a question and conduct a survey, showing results in a diagram

Challenge 1

Ask your class two questions about subjects at school.

Do you like English? Do you like Science?

Draw a Venn diagram of your results.

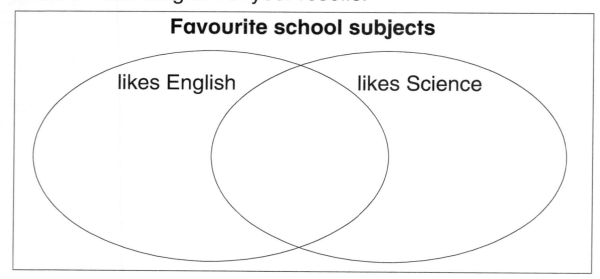

Favourite school subjects

likes English   likes Science

Challenge 2

1 Ask your class, collect data and make a pictogram of the results.

Favourite ice cream flavours	Total
chocolate	
strawberry	
vanilla	

= 1 child

chocolate	
strawberry	
vanilla	

2 Organise this survey information into a Venn diagram.

Favourite types of book

Boys	Girls
information	stories
stories	information
adventure	craft
sport	animal

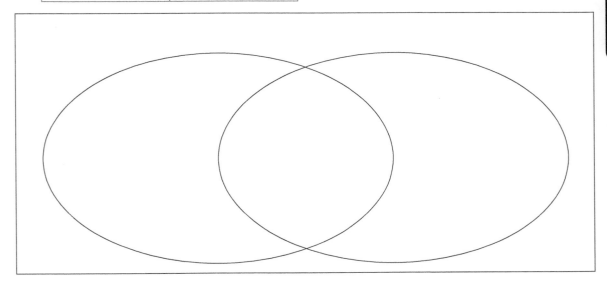

Challenge 3 Ask your class, collect the data and create a Carroll diagram.

Do you have a pet?

Do you have a brother?

	has a pet	does not have a pet
has a brother		
does not have a brother		

127

Notes